OUTLAWS
and
GUNFIGHTERS
of the Old West

by
Phillip W. Steele

PELICAN PUBLISHING COMPANY
Gretna 1998

First Pelican edition, 1998

Library of Congress Cataloging-in-Publication Data

Steele, Phillip W.
    Outlaws and gunfighters of the Old West / by Phillip W.
Steele. — 1st Pelican ed.
      p.   cm.
    Originally published: Springdale, AR : Heritage Publishers,
c1991.
    Includes bibliographical references.
    ISBN 1-56554-137-5 (pb : alk. paper)
    1. Outlaws—West (U.S.)—Biography. 2. Frontier and pioneer
life—West (U.S.) 3. West (U.S.)—Biography.   I. Title.
F594.S797 1998
364.15'52'092278—dc21   98-2613
                                                  CIP

Manufactured in the United States of America

Published by Pelican Publishing Company, Inc.
P.O. Box 3110, Gretna, Louisiana 70054-3110

Contents

		Page
	Acknowledgements	2
	Introduction	5
Chapter 1.	Jesse and Frank James	9
Chapter 2.	The Dalton Gang	29
Chapter 3.	John Wesley Hardin	57
Chapter 4.	Gunfight at the O.K. Corral	69
Chapter 5.	Belle Starr	87
Chapter 6.	Billy the Kid	105

Illustrations

Jesse and Frank James	10, 14, 17 20, 23, 25, 28
The Dalton Gang	30, 36, 45, 49, 53
John Wesley Hardin	56, 65
Gunfight at the O.K. Corral	70, 73, 76, 78, 79
Belle Starr	86, 88, 92, 96, 98 102, 104
Billy the Kid	106, 117

Acknowledgements

Numerous research sources and interviews with descendants and historians have been of great help to this author in the preparation of this text over the past two years. Various members of the National Outlaw and Lawman History Association were especially helpful in seeking to separate fact from legend. Sources which have been the most helpful are as follows.

Interviews and Research Assistance

Lee Baecher, Dalton family research
Lawrence H. Barr, Jesse James grandson
Thelma Duncan Barr, Jesse James family
Marley Brant, the Younger family
Kenneth Butler, Earp and Dalton research
Don Cline, Billy the Kid
Brookie Craig, Dalton family research
Joe Dalton, Dalton family research
Harold L. Edwards, Dalton research
Bill Livingston, Dalton family research
Leon Metz, Billy the Kid
Bill O'Neil, O.K. Corral
Ethel Rose Owens, Jesse James granddaughter
Milton F. Perry, Jesse and Frank James research
Veleska Ridley, Belle and Pearl Starr family
James R. Ross, Jesse James great-grandson
John Wesley Thompson, John Wesley Hardin family
Ben Traywick, Tombstone, Arizona
Flossie Mae Wiley, Belle and Pearl Starr family
Reba Earp Young, The Earp family

Magazines and Newspapers

Mike Flanagan, "O.K. Corral," *Denver Post Magazine*, 1984.

Sue Van Slyke, "Clantons," *NOLA Quarterly*, 1990.

Jim Dullenty, Robert Curry, "Wyatt Earp," *NOLA Quarterly*.

Phillip Rasch, "Billy the Kid," *NOLA Quarterly*, 1983.
David S. Elliott, "The Daltons," *Coffeyville Journal*, 1892.
A. J. Wright, "Hardin," *NOLA Quarterly*, 1982.
Wilfred P. Deac, "Billy the Kid," *Wild West*, 1991.
"Billy the Kid," *True West*, 1990.
"O. K. Corral," *Tombstone Epitaph*, 1881.
Mike Whye, "Stories Behind Legends," *Midwest Motorists*, 1991.
Bill O'Neil, "Aftermath of O. K. Corral," *Truewest*, 1991.

Books
Dr. William A. Settle, *Jesse James Was His Name*. University of Missouri Press
Carl W. Breihan, *The Man Who Shot Jesse James*. A. S. Barnes & Company
John Poe, *The Killing of Billy the Kid*. Frontier Press.
John Wesley Hardin, *The Life of John Wesley Hardin*. Univesity of Oklahoma Press.
Col. Charles Mooney, *Doctor in Belle Starr Country*. Century Press.
Donald R. Hale, *We Rode with Quantrill*.
Jerry J. Gaddy, *Dust to Dust*. Presidio Press.
Jay Robert Nash, *Bloodletters and Badmen*. M. Evans & Co.
David Stewart Elliott, *Last Raid of the Daltons*. Coffeyville Journal.
George Turner, *Gunfighters*. Baxter Lane Co.
John Tuska, *Billy the Kid*. University of Nebraska Press.
Robert Utley, *Billy the Kid*. University of Nebraska Press.
Emmett Dalton, *When the Daltons Rode*. Doubleday, Doran & Co.
Albert Pendleton, Susan Thomas, *In Search of the Hollidays*.

Institutions

Dalton Museum, Coffeyville, Kansas
Chisholm Trail Museum, Kingfisher, Oklahoma
James Farm Museum, Kearney, Missouri
Liberty Bank Museum, Liberty, Missouri

Judge Parker's Court National Park, Fort Smith, Arkansas
Old Fort Museum, Fort Smith, Arkansas
Oklahoma Historical Society, Oklahoma City, Oklahoma
Kansas Historical Society, Topeka, Kansas
Wyatt Earp Birthplace, Monmouth, Illinois
Coffeyville Kansas Library
Fort Smith Arkansas Library
Ottawa Kansas Library
Arizona Society of Pioneers, Phoenix, Arizona

Introduction

Numerous books, articles, and films about each of the outlaws and gunfighters to be discussed in the following chapters have been presented over the past century. Many such books, articles, and films have helped create these personalities and their significance in the history of the American West. although there have been several highly respected writers and researchers over the years attempt to present the true facts about these personalities and the events of historical significance in which they were involved, fictional accounts far exceed the few who presented non-fiction examinations of lives and events of Old West history.

The basic human need for entertainment before the development of radio, television, films, video, or the hundreds of other entertainment forms we enjoy today, created an endless demand for fictional novels with an Old West setting. Early fiction writers therefore attempted to fill this demand by turning out their pulp westerns in the volume to meet their publisher's deadlines. Most such novels were created only from the writer's imagination with little concern for investigating true facts. Such pulp westerns often used real personalities and real events in their plots but were created only to satisfy the reader's demand for excitement. Such novel glamorization of various personalities and events therefore often distorted the true story and resulted in creating many heros and heroins that not necessarily deserve the place in western history bestowed upon them. Such pulp novelists and their work should not necessarily be criticized as many were literary masterpieces written only for the purpose of entertaining their loyal readers. The noted outlaw Frank James once commented about such fictional novels, "I found one of those cheap novels about me and Jesse. There is no truth in them, and they should not be sold to young boys of today. We won't let our son Robbie read them. The one I found was about us robbing a train. It's sickening to read how Jesse bragged about what he had done. I never heard Jess ever brag about who he was or what he did. A lot of robberies blamed on me and Jesse we never did." Such novels, however, helped to create many of the personalities we are to examine in the following pages.

This writer has attempted to separate facts from the volumes of fiction to determine the true story of each personality and event presented here. Hundreds of documents, newspaper accounts, respected past authors and known authorities on these personalities and events have been studied and interviewed in preparing *Outlaws and Gunfighters*. Numerous descendants of the James, Younger, Belle Starr, Dalton, Hardin, Earp, and Holliday families have also been interviewed in our search for the true story. Such family member oral history often proves to be the best source for accuracy. Although extreme concern for accuracy has been followed, it is often impossible to totally separate facts from the volumes of fiction previously reported. It is hoped, however, that those accounts presented here will prove to be as historically accurate as possible and that the reader will find these true stories of outlaws and gunfighters to be even more interesting than the past fictional misrepresentations.

This writer first met John D. LeVan, III in Tulsa, Oklahoma. A country blues guitarist, LeVan was found to have an inbred feeling and love for true history of America's Old West. His grandfather, Harry Miller LeVan, often told his family of his experiences with the Dalton gang at an early age. The son of John D. LeVan the first, a money lender in Coffeyville, Kansas, Harry Miller LeVan became friends with the Dalton family during their few years as neighbors on farms near Coffeyville. Learning of the Daltons plans to rob the two banks in Coffeyville simultaneously, Harry Miller LeVan rode to their camp where he attempted to convince his friends of the foolishness of their plans. LeVan's pleas went unheard.

LeVan later became associated with Waite Phillips, founder of the Phillips 66 Oil Company in Bartlesville. Through his influence, LeVan helped his old friend Emmett Dalton get a pardon from his life sentence in the Kansas State Penitentiary after serving fifteen years.

Not only did John D. LeVan share this writer's deep interest in the Dalton story, but also in Old West history in general. Our common Cancerian birth sign further created our common interest in LeVan's music interpretations. Provided with the true facts about the lives and personalities presented in this text, LeVan composed music and lyrics that also tell the true stories on the original album created to accompany this book.

Recorded by Lane Audio Productions, who also shared our interest in the Old West, musicians

Tommy McClelland, Sunny LeVan, Rick Eby, and Mark Vanderhoof assisted in creating these unique and historically accurate musical accounts. This author and musician John D. LeVan sincerely hope that this book and album presentation will not only prove to be entertaining and educational but also be recognized as an attempt to preserve our nation's western history for future generations.

Phillip W. Steele

Chapter 1

Jesse and Frank James

Jesse Woodson James

Alexander Franklin James

Without question Jesse James tops the list of personalities featured in the annals of western history and folklore. More books, films, and television shows have been written and produced about Jesse James and his brother Frank than any other personalities found in literature of the American West. A few years ago a survey was taken throughout Europe on the most recognizable names of famous Americans. Surprisingly, above all presidents in our history, Mickey Mouse was at the top of the list. Not surprisingly, Jesse James was second. One might wonder just why it is that Jesse James, a noted outlaw, obtained such international popularity which has endured for over a century. There are no doubt several reasons for this.

Not only was his name, Jesse James, somewhat romantic; but also the fact that he and his older brother Frank James were successful in eluding capture by law authorities for some seventeen years, further contributed to their popularity. John Newman Edwards, the founder of the *Kansas City Star* newspaper had served as a major in the Confederate army and was sympathetic toward the Confederate cause long after the end of the Civil War. Jesse and Frank James had also served the Confederacy in the ranks of William Clarke Quantrill's guerrilla forces. Edwards perhaps first created the public interest in the exploits of the James brothers through his romantic editorials that appeared regularly in his newspaper. Such articles not only created the Robin Hood image for Jesse by promoting the legend of his robbing from the rich and giving to the poor, but also attempted to justify the James boys' many crimes. History has proven that the James brothers seldom, if ever, only robbed from the rich and gave to the poor. The fact that most all of their crimes were carried out against institutions controlled or operated by federal interests is true. Quantrill guerrilla veterans were prevented from ever re-establishing their rightful place in society after the Civil War. Federal law prevented such veterans from ever holding public office; and, they could no longer vote, could not borrow money from a bank, or even be a member of a church. Such restrictions became a controversial case of American civil rights which brought further public interest to the James brothers. All of this and the romantic promotion of their daring exploits Edwards created in his editorials provided early dime novel writers with material from which their hundreds of fiction novels were written. Such a volume of literature no doubt helped place the James brothers at the top of the popularity list in western history. Their popularity remains today as new publications featuring James history continue to be released annually.

Robert Sallee James, father of the James brothers, was one of eight children born to John and Amanda James in Logan County, Kentucky. Robert was born July 17, 1818. Robert attended Georgetown College in Georgetown, Kentucky where he studied to become a Baptist minister. He entered Georgetown College in 1839 and graduated in 1843. He then returned to Georgetown periodically for graduate study and received his Masters degree in 1847.

Robert met Zerelda Elizabeth Cole at a revival meeting in Stamping Ground, Kentucky. Zerelda was the daughter of James Cole and Sallie Lindsay Cole of Midway, Kentucky. Cole operated an inn and tavern on the old Lexington-Frankfort Road known as the Blackhorse Tavern. James Cole was killed in a horse accident when Zerelda was young. Her mother then married Robert Thomason and, along with Zerelda's brother Jesse Richard Cole, moved to Clay County, Missouri. Zerelda remained in Stamping Ground, Kentucky under the guardianship of her uncle, James Lindsay.

Zerelda entered St. Catherine's Academy, a Catholic school for girls in Georgetown in 1840. After a brief courtship, Robert James and Zerelda married on December 28, 1841 in her uncle James Lindsay's home in Stamping Ground, Kentucky. Soon afterward, the couple moved to Clay County, Missouri, where Zerelda resided with her mother and stepfather Robert Thomason while Robert James returned to Kentucky to finish graduate study at Georgetown. Alexander Franklin James, their first son, was born in Missouri January 10, 1843, while Robert was away.

Returning to Missouri after his graduate study was completed, Robert acquired a 275 acre farm near the Kearney community in Clay County. There his second child, Robert, who only lived one month, was born July 19, 1845. Robert and Zerelda's third child, Jesse Woodson James, was born September 5, 1847 and their last child, Susan Lavenia, was born November 25, 1849.

Robert soon became a successful farmer in the region and also a popular Baptist minister. He founded two Baptist churches in Clay County that are still in existence today, and he was one of the

Zerelda Elizabeth Cole James

Zerelda James and Granddaughter Marry Barr on lawn of James Farm home

original founders of William Jewell College in Liberty, Missouri. When gold was discovered in California in 1849, Robert joined thousands of others on the gold rush. Hoping to gain sufficient wealth to provide a good education for his family and to help expand his Baptist missionary dreams, Robert left his family in 1850. His dreams were not to be realized, for soon after his arrival Robert died of food poisoning in a Placerville, California gold camp and was buried in an unmarked grave.

Zerelda James then married Benjamin Simms, a neighboring farmer. Simms was accidentally killed a short time later.

Zerelda then married Dr. Reuben Samuel on September 25, 1855. Frank James was age twelve, Jesse age eight, and Susan James only six years of age at the time. Dr. Samuel became the only father the James children ever knew and a close relationship was developed between them.

As were most Kentucky families, the James and Samuel families were slave owners and were strong advocates for the Confederate cause when the War Between the States began in 1861. Frank James joined the Confederate army. Captured after the battle of Wilsons Creek near Springfield, Missouri, Frank was forced to take a pledge supporting the Union. He was then released and he returned home. Shortly thereafter Frank left home and joined the band of Missouri irregular forces under the command of an ex-school teacher from Kansas, William Clarke Quantrill. The Quantrill guerrilla forces soon became the bloodiest fighting force in the Civil War.

Jesse James, barely sixteen years of age as the

war began, was too young to enlist and remained with his family at their Clay County farm home. While plowing the fields one day in 1864, young Jesse was surrounded by a party of Federal soldiers. Refusing to answer when repeatedly ask about the location of his brother and Quantrill's camp, the party severely whipped Jesse with bull whips. Crawling to his house after the beating, Jesse found his stepfather Dr. Samuel had been hanged from a tree near his house and his mother was trying to get him down. Dr. Samuel did not die from the hanging but lack of oxygen to his brain caused by the hanging effected him mentally thereafter. The tragic events of that day no doubt greatly contributed to Jesse James' bitterness toward the Union and his choosing to continue seeking vengeance long after the Civil War.

Jesse immediately left to join his brother Frank and Quantrill. Quantrill reluctantly accepted young Jesse, then only sixteen years of age, into their ranks. Serving under Quantrill's lieutenant Bloody Bill Anderson, Jesse's bitterness and his ability as a marksman soon earned him respect throughout Quantrill's band.

As the war drew to an end, Frank James chose to ride with a Quantrill party into Kentucky and was with Quantrill when he was mortally wounded in a skirmish at Wakefield, Kentucky in 1865. Frank James surrendered at Stamping Ground, Kentucky soon after and returned to Missouri.

Jesse James had ridden with a party into Texas as the war drew to a close. Returning to Missouri, the band approached a Federal garrison at Lexington, Missouri under a white flag, planning to

William Clarke Quantrill

Jesse James in Guerilla uniform

surrender. The party was suddenly fired upon by the Federals. Jesse received severe wounds in his chest and leg in the skirmish. Returning home to recuperate, Jesse must have made decisions to continue fighting those who had so tragically interfered with his life and family, for he was never known to officially surrender again after being wounded in his first surrender attempt.

Finding much of their family farm destroyed and severe economic conditions forced upon them as a result of their Quantrill association, the James brothers, along with several other former Quantrill associates, decided to fight back. On February 13, 1866 a group of some ten or more, including Jesse and Frank James, Jim, Bob, John and Cole Younger made national newspaper headlines by robbing the Clay County Savings Bank in Liberty, Missouri of some $60,000. This was the first daytime bank robbery in peacetime in America. Thus the James-Younger gang first gained notoriety.

Since the James-Younger gang was receiving the most publicity in newspapers around the nation, the gang was accused of numerous robberies and various crimes they did not do. Robberies credited to them by history are described here.

In March of 1868 Jesse and Frank went to their uncle George Hite's home near Adairville, Kentucky for a visit. While there a gang believed to have been led by the James brothers robbed the Norton and Long Bank of Russellville, Kentucky on March 20. The gang's third bank robbery was of the Gallatin, Missouri bank on December 7, 1869. A citizen, John Sheets, was killed during the Gallatin robbery. On July 3, 1871 the gang traveled to Iowa where the bank of Corydon was robbed of $14,000.

Thousands were attending the Kansas City state fair when a party believed to be the James-Younger gang robbed the fair office of $10,000. Their next robbery was of the St. Genevive, Missouri bank on May 27, 1873, in which $6,100 was taken. A stagecoach was stopped by the gang between Malvern and Hot Springs, Arkansas on January 15, 1874 and $4,000 taken.

The nation's first train robbery was credited to the gang when the Rock Island train was robbed of $3,000 near Adair, Iowa on July, 21, 1873. An engineer was killed during the robbery. A second stage coach robbery near Austin, Texas on April 7, 1874 brought the gang $3,000. Their second train robbery took place near Muncie, Kansas in December 1875 and earned the gang $55,000. Their last train robbery took place on July 7, 1876 when $15,000 was taken from the train at Rocky Cut, Missouri. While living in Tennessee the James gang took $5,200 from a Federal paymaster near Muscle Shoals, Alabama on March 11, 1881.

On April 24, 1874 Jesse James married Zerelda Amanda Mimms. Zerelda, referred to as Zee, was his first cousin and was named after his mother. They were married by Jesse's uncle William James in Zee's sister's home in Kearney, Missouri.

Frank James married Anna Ralston, from a prominent Missouri family, some two months after Jesse's marriage on June 6, 1874.

Public sentiment supporting the James brothers was greatly increased on the evening of January 26, 1875. Apparently given information by Jack Ladd, a farm hand employee of Daniel Askew's farm

*The Youngers, Bob, Jim, and Cole with their sister
Henrietta. Photo was made in the Minnesota State Prison.*

which bordered the James farm, Pinkerton detectives thought Jesse and Frank James were at home and formed a party to capture them. Surrounding the house, a flare was thrown through the window to light up the room. Dr. and Mrs. Samuel rushed in. Seeing the burning device they quickly pushed the flare into the fireplace with a poker. As it reached the fire the flare exploded. A fragment tore a large hole in the side of nine year old Archie Samuel who was sleeping nearby. He died within an hour. Zerelda Samuel's right hand was mangled so badly that it was necessary to amputate her right arm at the elbow. This one event not only greatly contributed to the future direction of Jesse and Frank James but the tragic attack on the family resulting in an old lady being badly injured and an innocent young boy killed caused great criticism for the Pinkerton led lawmen in Missouri.

Realizing that the large rewards posted for the James-Younger gang throughout the nation would soon end their outlaw activities, they created a plan to assume aliases, move to Tennessee and, hopefully, become peaceful citizens and raise their families. They needed only one more large stake to finance their plans. The bank in Northfield, Minnesota was believed to be quite wealthy and was managed by a former Federal officer who had caused the James family so many problems during the war. On September 7, 1876 Jesse and Frank James, Cole, Bob, and Jim Younger, Clell Miller, Charlie Pitts, and Bill Chadwell attempted to rob Northfield's First National Bank. During the attempt Miller, Pitts, and Chadwell were killed. Cole, Bob, and Jim Younger were all seriously wounded, captured and given lengthy prison terms in the Minnesota State prison. Only Jesse and Frank James escaped.

Highly sought after throughout the nation, Jesse made arrangements to take his wife Zee to the hill country of Tennessee near the Waverly community. There he took the alias of John Davis Howard and attempted to earn a living as a horse dealer. While in Waverly, twin sons, Gould and Montgomery, whom they had named after two doctors in the region, were stillborn. Soon afterward Jesse moved to Nashville where he first resided in a home on Hydes Ferry Road with his brother Frank and his wife Annie. Frank had earlier moved to Nashville where he took the name of Ben J. Woodson.

Jesse and Zee's son Jesse Edwards was born on August 31, 1875 in the Edgehill region of Nashville. The boy was named in honor of John Newman Edwards, the Kansas City newspaper man who had treated the James brothers kindly in his editorials and also contributed to their notoriety. A daughter, Mary Susan, was also born in Nashville on June 17, 1879. Frank and Annie James' only child, Robert Franklin, was born in Nashville February 6, 1878.

While in Nashville, Frank was employed as a tenant farmer, a wooden bucket salesman, and for the Indiana Lumber Company. Jesse earned a living as a horse buyer and both Frank and Jesse were regular participants in horse racing throughout the Tennessee and Kentucky region under their Howard and Woodson aliases during their few years in Nashville.

On March 25, 1881, Tom Ryan, an outlaw associate of the James-Younger gang who knew the James brothers well in Nashville, was arrested in a

Zerelda (Zee) James, wife of Jesse James with their children Jesse Edwards and Mary Susan.

saloon at White's Creek near Nashville and taken to the Nashville jail. As soon as they learned of Ryan's capture, not trusting what Ryan might say, both Jesse and Frank left Nashville with their families. Frank took his wife and child to Virginia. Jesse, Zee, and their children returned to Missouri. After spending a few weeks with Zee's family in Kansas City, Jesse, under the name of Tom Howard, rented a house in St. Joseph, Missouri on Christmas Eve of 1881.

Jesse noticed a classified ad in a Kansas City newspaper offering a Nebraska farm for sale. Once again, needing a nest egg, what was to be his final robbery was planned. Finally, after eluding the law for some seventeen years, he hoped to obtain enough cash to buy the Nebraska farm where he could raise his family in peace. Most all of the former James-Younger gang associates were, by now, either dead or in prison and there were few Jesse felt he could trust.

Robert Newton Ford had ridden with Jesse and Frank on a few occasions. Ford had secretly negotiated with Clay County Sheriff and Missouri Governor Thomas Crittenden a plan to finally bring down the notorious Jesse James for the $10,000 reward being offered for him. Trusting Ford, Jesse invited him to his St. Joseph home to help him plan a robbery of the Platte City, Missouri bank. Ford was successful in convincing Jesse to let his brother Charlie Ford, though inexperienced, assist them in the robbery.

On the morning of April 3, 1882 Jesse had breakfast with his wife Zee, their two children, and the Ford brothers. Leaving the kitchen table, Jesse

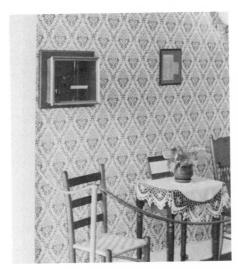

Site where Jesse James was killed by Bob Ford in St. Joseph, Missouri on April 3, 1882.

Robert Newton Ford

walked into the parlor. Since it was a warm spring morning he raised the normally drawn window shades and then raised the window to let fresh spring air into the stuffy parlor. Jesse then removed his coat and gun belt and laid it across a daybed. The morning sunlight flooding the room clearly reflected an accumulation of dust on a wall picture that also needed straightening. Jesse then picked up a feather duster and stood on a chair to dust and straighten the picture. Just why Jesse James, who was never known to remove his gun belt when others were present, did so when the Ford brothers were present has been continually debated by James historians over the last century. At the moment the unarmed Jesse stepped upon the chair, Bob Ford pulled his pistol and fired. The bullet struck Jesse below the right ear and lodged in his left temple. Jesse James fell to the floor dead.

Jesse's body was taken by his family to Kearney, Missouri by train. After his funeral the body was buried on the lawn of the James farm. There Zerelda James felt it could be carefully watched and protected from grave robbers and souvenir hunters. When Jesse's wife Zee died in 1902, Jesse's grave was disintered and the remains re-buried alongside those of his wife in the Mt. Olivet cemetery in Kearney, Missouri.

Frank James made arrangements through John Newman Edwards to surrender to Governor Thomas Crittenden in Jefferson City, Missouri on October 5, 1882. Frank was first tried for the death of John Sheets during the robbery of the Gallatin bank. He was acquitted. Next he was tried by authorities in Alabama for the robbery of a paymaster in Muscle

Shoals, Alabama which was credited to the James gang during their years in Nashville. Once again, Frank was acquitted. Frank, now a national celebrity, was in demand for promoting various events such as fairs, horse racing events, and other such public affairs. He also was solicited to promote various products. He worked for a period promoting a shoe manufacturing business in Nevada, Missouri. He also promoted a large department store chain in Dallas, Texas and spent several years as the race starter for Oak Lawn race track in Hot Springs, Arkansas. In 1909 Frank purchased a horse ranch near Fletcher, Oklahoma and moved his family there.

Annie James was accompanying Frank's mother Zerelda on a train trip back to Missouri after her visit in Fletcher when Zerelda suffered a fatal heart attack near Oklahoma City on February 10, 1911. Upon his mother's death, Frank James returned his family to Missouri where he was to spend the rest of his life at the James farm. Frank died of natural causes at age seventy-two on February 15, 1915. His body was cremated and his ashes stored in a Kearney bank until the death of Annie on July 6, 1944. Annie was buried in the Hill Park cemetery in Independence, Missouri. Shortly thereafter the ashes of her husband Frank James were buried alongside Annie's grave.

Robert and Charlie Ford, now somewhat celebrities for bringing down the notorious Jesse James, traveled for a few months with a theatrical company where they reenacted their assassination of Jesse James. They were often booed off the stage by the audience. Charlie Ford, becoming despondent over his and Bob Ford's ridicule by the public, finally committed suicide.

Bob Ford, with the reward money received for his action, first went to Las Vegas, Nevada where he opened a saloon. The public avoided his establishment. He then moved to Pueblo, Colorado where he once again opened a saloon business. In Pueblo he had his first altercation with Ed O'Kelley, a member of the Pueblo police force who openly ridiculed Bob Ford for the cowardly manner in which he shot the unarmed Jesse James in the back of the head.

A large tent city developed rapidly in Creede, Colorado when a major gold strike was made there. Ford left Pueblo and opened a tent saloon in Creede. On the morning of June 8, 1892 Ed O'Kelley entered Ford's saloon, pulled out his double-barrel sawed-off shotgun from his coat and fired both barrels into Ford's head.

Jesse James in Death

Chapter 2

The Dalton Gang

Coffeyville citizens holding the bodies of Grat Dalton, left, and Bob Dalton after the Dalton's unsuccessful attempt to rob two Coffeyville banks simultaneously on October 5, 1892.

James Lewis Dalton, Jr. was born in Mt. Sterling, Kentucky on February 16, 1826. The following year he moved with his parents to Jackson County, Missouri. There he attended school and helped his father on their family farm. At age twenty James Lewis enlisted in the army on June 9, 1846 to serve in the Mexican War. He served with a Fifer Company in the Second Kentucky Infantry until he was discharged in New Orleans on June 9, 1847. Returning to Missouri he obtained employment as a saloon keeper. Various members of the Charles Lee Younger family frequented Dalton's saloon and through this association he met Adeline Lee Younger, one of Charles Lee Younger's seventeen children from Lee Summit, Missouri. James Lewis and Adeline were married in Jackson County, Missouri on March 12, 1851. Adeline's half brother, Henry Washington Younger, was the father of Coleman, Bob, Jim, and John Younger who later gained national notoriety as members of the James-Younger Gang.

Adeline's father left her two hundred and ten acres in Cass County, Missouri in his will of February 26, 1852. The Daltons then moved to the Cass County farm. There the following children were born to James Lewis and Adeline:

Charles Benjamin	Feb. 24, 1852
Henry Coleman	1854
Louis Kossuth	1855
Littleton Lee	1858
Franklin	1859
Gratten Hanley	1861
William Mason	1863
Eva Mae	June 25, 1867

Robert Renick	1869
Emmett	May 3, 1871
Leona	July 1875
Nancy May	March 11, 1876
Simon Noel	1879

In 1880 James Lewis moved his family to a farm in Labette County, Kansas some eight miles north of the Coffeyville, Kansas community. During the some three years the Daltons lived near Coffeyville, they became familiar to most of the city's citizens. John D. LeVan was a money lender associated with the Condon Bank in Coffeyville for many years. Harry Miller LeVan, son of John D. LeVan, became good friends with the Dalton boys during the few years the Dalton family were neighbors to the LeVans. James Lewis Dalton, resulting from his common overindulgence in whisky and his continual conflicts over his heavy gambling, was often in trouble and jailed by Coffeyville authorities. Pressure coming to bear from the Coffeyville community not wanting the Daltons in their city resulted in the family moving once again in 1882. They went to Indian Territory where they leased farm land a short distance from the Vinita community. James Lewis continued his restless lifestyle. Drinking and gambling heavily, Dalton followed the horse race circuit around the region. Seldom home, Adeline Dalton was found alone on their Indian territory farm most of the time with her large family.

Adeline's cousins, the Youngers, were shot to pieces and given lengthy prison terms for attempting to rob the First National Bank in Northfield,

Minnesota on September 7, 1876. Jesse James was killed by Bob Ford on April 3, 1882. Although their mother Adeline strongly disapproved of her cousin's outlaw activities and attempted to prevent her children from reading the dime novels of the day glamorizing the James-Younger Gang, the Dalton boys no doubt were proud of their relationship to the notorious Youngers. Such admiration may have contributed to the young Dalton boys dreams of also developing national notoriety to equal or surpass that of their Younger cousins.

The Cherokee Strip Indian Lands in the western part of Indian Territory were opened for settlement in 1889. Adeline loaded up her belongings and with her family joined the thousands who made the land run to claim lands in the new territory. Her now estranged husband, James Lewis, followed but died suddenly along the trail near the Dearing, Kansas community. He was buried there in an unmarked grave with little, if any, sentiment from his estranged family.

Adeline settled on land some six miles from the community of Kingfisher. They first built a sod dug-out home and later a log cabin. In 1892 Cheyenne-Arapahoe lands were also opened for settlement a few miles to the west. Adeline sent her son Simon to also claim land there.

Needless to mention, Adeline was faced with many hardships trying to raise her thirteen children alone in Indian Territory. She was an accomplished seamstress and attempted to provide for her family by taking in sewing while her boys helped with the farm chores. Devoutly religious, Adeline tried to raise her children to be honest and upright citizens and made sure they attended school and church activities.

Ben, Henry, and Littleton Dalton left to find opportunities in California. William Mason, "Bill", Dalton also left at an early age to join his brothers in California. There Bill met and married Jane Blevins, the daughter of the politically prominent W. B. Blevins. Very likeable and outspoken against the railroads, Bill Dalton also became politically popular. He was elected to serve in the California state legislature and was even considered as a possible candidate for governor through the influence of his father-in-law.

Frank Dalton, being extremely familiar with Indian Territory, rode to Fort Smith, Arkansas where he was appointed as a Deputy United States Marshall to serve Judge Isaac Parker's Federal Court. Records indicate that Frank Dalton performed his duties as a law officer well and may have influenced or at least helped his brothers Bob and Grat Dalton to also become law officers for a period. On November 30, 1887 deputy marshalls Frank Dalton and James R. Cole were assigned to seek out an outlaw Dave Smith and bring him back to Fort Smith to answer the many charges against him. Locating Smith's camp some fifty miles west of Fort Smith, the two lawmen dismounted their horses and quietly approached a large tent in which Smith and several of his outlaw associates were dining and drinking heavily. As Dalton stepped into the tent, Smith arose from the table, pulled his gun, and fired a bullet into Dalton's chest. Deputy Cole then immediately killed Smith. Others in the tent fled rapidly but continued to fire at Cole as they ran.

Cole was wounded six times but not seriously. Cole's return fire mortally wounded one of the outlaws known only as Dixon. Deputy Marshall Frank Dalton was seriously wounded by Smith but was still alive. One of the outlaws, believed to have been William Towerly, ran to where Dalton lay and pointed his pistol at Dalton's head. Dalton pleaded with the outlaw to let him live to no avail. Towerley's shot split open Dalton's head. Adeline Dalton and one of her sons went to Fort Smith to claim Frank's body. They then took the body to Coffeyville, Kansas where Frank was buried in the Dalton family plot in the Elmwood cemetery. The grave was not to be marked until Emmett Dalton returned to Coffeyville in 1924. Frank Dalton's monument, which Emmett had erected, records his death as being November 27, 1888 when it was actually in 1887.

Before leaving Vinita, Indian Territory, Bob Dalton and his brother Grat served as deputy marshals with the Osage police in the Osage Nation. They were often also called on by their respected brother Frank Dalton, a deputy U. S. Marshall, to assist him in tracking down known criminals in the territory. Bob and Grat being somewhat dishonest in the performance of their lawmen duties often took advantage of the badges they wore. During this period Bob and Grat, sometimes also accompanied by brother Emmett, used their position to steal horses and commit other petty crimes. Florence "Flo" Quick has often been mentioned in Dalton history as serving as a fence and marketplace for the horses the Daltons managed to accumulate and bring to her in Baxter Springs, Kansas. Emmett Dalton, though considerably younger than his

Emmett

Bob

Frank

Grat

Bill

The Daltons

brothers Bob and Grat, admired his lawman brothers and often rode with them.

Several stories exist as to how the Daltons first met the Wesley "Tex" Johnson family. Although Emmett was to later mention in his book *When The Dalton's Rode* that he first met Julia Johnson when she was playing an organ in a church in 1887, he may also have met the family earlier.

Shortly before leaving Vinita in 1889, Bob, Grat, and younger brother Emmett came upon a wagon in which Wesley Johnson was moving his family through Indian Territory. Surrounded by a party of renegade Indians who were attempting to rob the Johnsons, the Dalton boys scattered the Indians and rescued the Johnsons. Irregardless of just how the Daltons first met the Johnsons, the two families were to have a close and long relationship thereafter. The Johnsons settled near the Copan community near the Kansas border. Apparently visiting the Johnsons often, Bob Dalton was known to have had a love affair with Lucy Johnson. Later in life, after serving some fifteen years in the Kansas State Prison, Emmett Dalton would marry Julia Johnson.

Although Adeline, the family matriarch constantly pleaded with her sons to give up their questionable activities and settle down to be simple farmers, the apparent restless spirit inherited from their father prevailed. Continuing their horse stealing activities around the territory under the guise as lawmen, it was not to be long until their charade would be discovered. Their pretense at being lawmen ended in June of 1890. Highly suspected of numerous crimes around the territory, the Daltons decided to leave the territory. Ben Canty, a former neighbor to the Daltons in Missouri, was now the town marshall in Silver City, New Mexico. Canty had a reputation of being tolerant with his town resulting in a wide-open, good-time city full of gambling halls and beautiful girls. The Daltons therefore decided to take a long needed vacation from their combined lawmen and outlaw activities in the territory.

They found Silver City all they had heard it to be. After several weeks of relaxing around the town, drinking and gambling, the Daltons were preparing to leave but hoped to have one last big night at the gambling tables to finance their trip home. It was a bad night for them at the tables, however, and they left with their pockets empty. Upset about the saloon taking all their money and deciding they had been cheated by crooked dealers, what may have been the Dalton's first armed robbery was committed. Returning to the saloon, they pulled their guns and demanded several sacks be filled with cash from the gambling tables. A posse was hurriedly formed by their old friend Marshall Ben Canty which would chase the Daltons hundreds of miles as they ran back to Indian territory. Thus the Daltons first made newspaper headlines which, especially their leader Bob, no doubt embellished. Not only had they satisfied themselves by revenging the saloon that had cheated them, but also were living up to their Younger family heritage.

Their questionable activities as lawmen in Indian Territory and news of their New Mexico armed robbery resulted in the Daltons becoming wanted men. Realizing their future in Indian

Territory was now gone, and no longer being able to call upon their respected brother Deputy Marshall Frank, they had only one place to turn, their respected brothers in California. Bob, Grat, and younger brother Emmett then left the family in Kingfisher and traveled to California where they hoped their respected brothers Littleton, Bill, and Henry would help them start a new life. Brother Ben had earlier returned to live with his mother in Kingfisher.

Brother Bill, now a highly respected politician because of his outspoken oratory against the atrocities of the railroad empire, welcomed his brothers and encouraged them to put aside their Indian Territory reputation to seek respectable labor. Bob and Grat no doubt accepted their brother's advice and may have had honest plans to become respectable farmers in California. Bill's strong feelings against the railroads, the fact they still embellished their Younger family relationship, and need to finance a respectable future, the Daltons chose to make a final surprise train robbery.

The Southern Pacific train # 17 left Alila, California at 7:50 p.m. on February 6, 1891. Two masked men surprised Engineer J. P. Thorne and Fireman G. S. Radcliffe by entering the train cab a short distance down the track with pistols drawn. Stopping the train and using Thorne and Radcliffe as shields, they walked to the express car and demanded the Express Guard Haswell to open the car. Haswell refused and opened fire on the bandits through the door. A brief and lively gunfight ensued in the darkness which resulted in Haswell receiving a minor wound in the head and Radcliffe being shot through the body. Realizing the hopelessness of their robbery attempt the Daltons fled. The train then continued on to Delano where Tulare County Sheriff Eugene Kay was notified of the robbery by telegraph. Haswell received medical attention and treatment was administered to Radcliffe; however, he died the next day.

Sheriff Kay rushed to Visalia with deputies Witty and Overall. There they were met by Sheriff Borgwardt of Kern County and a posse was formed. Tracking the bandits for several days, the trail led to the home of Bill Dalton some thirteen miles east of the Paso Robles community. The Daltons hid nearby while the posse searched Bill Dalton's farm for evidence. A piece of saddle leather had been found near the train robbery site. Finding a saddle in Bill Dalton's barn matching the leather piece, it was evident that Bill Dalton was somehow involved. A posse then combed the Coast Range Mountains for the Daltons. Bob and Emmett, realizing they had little chance of being acquitted if captured, and perhaps somewhat embarrassed over the problems they had caused their respectable brother Bill, decided to return to their familiar Indian Territory. Riding to Ludlow, California to board a train east, they abandoned their horses there. These horses were later identified as being at the Vasalia robbery.

Grat Dalton had been on the train when Bob and Emmett attempted to rob it, but left the train at Delano. There he waited for the next train to Fresno. Arriving in Fresno, law officers were waiting and arrested him.

Irregardless of Bill Dalton's political respectability, the fact he had been so anti-railroad in his political campaigns and horses were traced to his farm, Bill was also arrested.

Grat came to trial first. Since he was not actually seen at the robbery, all evidence was circumstantial. After some eighteen hours of deliberation the jury found Grat guilty and he was jailed. It was not long however until Grat escaped. Managing to systematically saw through the jail bars over a period of several days, on Sunday, September 26, 1891, an especially lax security day at the jail, Grat removed the bars and escaped with two other prisoners. Grat immediately headed for Indian Territory. Bill Dalton, who may have been aware of his brothers' train robbery plans, was at least not with them. Evidence found at Bill's ranch was not sufficient to convict him and, with the help of his influential father-in-law, charges against Bill were eventually dropped.

As a result of the Daltons' bungled California train robbery attempt, the Daltons were featured in newspaper headlines around the nation for the first time. Calling to mind once again their proud relationship to the Youngers, the Daltons, especially their leader Bob, no doubt enjoyed this publicity.

Little, if any, opportunity existed back in Indian Territory for making an honest livelihood. Feeling somewhat lucky, embarrassed, and embittered about their unsuccessful California trip, many campfire discussions were no doubt held regarding their future plans. Now broke, their lawman brother Frank dead, and reputations of being dishonest lawmen in the past, they had no place to turn.

Needing a stake to finance their future, whatever that may have been, their thoughts turned to bank robbery. The newspaper headlines and romantic editorials that had appeared after their Silver City saloon robbery and their California fiasco had elevated the Dalton name to some extent into the realm of folk heroism. The general population of the country sympathized with the revenge these poor farm boys had taken on the disreputable Silver City saloon. Railroads were generally hated for their greedy land confiscations. The Daltons, although now wanted by the law, were excused and supported by the general public. The vain Bob Dalton embellished his new notoriety and became the outspoken leader of the Dalton Gang.

Back in Indian Territory the Daltons looked up their old friends from cow punching days, Bill Doolin, Dick Broadwell, Black Faced Charlie Bryant, and Bill Power. Under the leadership of Bob Dalton, they began making plans. They first raided a colony of Missourians on Beaver Creek near Orlando. Eight or nine horses were stolen. A posse was quickly organized which followed them to Twin Mounds. The ensuing fight with the posse there resulted in the death of W. T. Starmer, one of the possemen.

The gang then once again turned to train robbery. On the night of June 1, 1892, the Daltons concealed themselves near the Santa Fe Depot in Red Rock, an Indian trading station in the Cherokee Strip. When the train stopped there at 9 o'clock, Broadwell and Charlie Bryant entered the locomotive while Grat Dalton and Bill Doolin forced the express car agent to open a safe containing several thousand dollars. Bob Dalton, Emmett Dalton and Bill Power herded the passengers onto the depot platform and robbed them. A telegraph operator was killed during this robbery.

The following July the Daltons robbed a Missouri, Kansas, and Texas passenger train near the community of Adair in the eastern part of the territory. Several Indian police guarding the train were wounded during the robbery and a physician passenger was killed.

Banks, perhaps even more so than the railroads, were hated by the general population. The Daltons cousins, the Youngers, along with Jesse and Frank James, had directed their past efforts toward major bank robberies. Brought down in their final attempt to rob a fat bank in Northfield, Minnesota, the James-Younger Gang had earned nationwide notoriety. Dime novels were by now regularly featuring the Youngers in their romantic episodes. No doubt by now depressed over their past failures and difficulty of living up to their relatives' reputation, the Daltons made bold plans.

Coffeyville, Kansas had been home to the Daltons for several years during their youth. Though their father James Lewis Dalton, Jr. had neglected his family most of his life, his sons still held some respect for the man. Treated badly by the local sheriff in Coffeyville and by the citizens of the city, the Dalton boys perhaps blamed such citizens for their father's downfall. Three reasons for choosing Coffeyville for their future plans therefore existed. They needed to make a large haul and Coffeyville being a booming border city had two full banks. Secondly, the city had treated their family unkindly during their years there and deserved to be repaid. Thirdly, and perhaps the most driving force, was that of Bob Dalton's ego. They embellished what little notoriety they had received. Certainly no one, not even the James Younger Gang, had ever successfully robbed two banks simultaneously. Familiar with Coffeyville and the fact their two banks, the Condon and First National, were only across the street from each other, a successful raid on both of them would not only be easy but gain the Dalton family a place in history to far exceed anything ever attempted by their Younger cousins.

Their thoughts also may have been of their beloved mother, Adeline, struggling for survival on her claim near Kingfisher. Their brothers Ben, who was mentally handicapped and irresponsible, and Simon, largely depended upon their handicapped sister Leona and mother Adeline for support through their meager earnings as seamstresses. Adeline and Leona also supported Nancy Dalton's son Roy Clute after Nancy's untimely death. Dreams of taking not only revenge on Coffeyville but also of obtaining sufficient wealth for their future no doubt contributed to their plans for Coffeyville which were developed over several weeks of campfire discussion.

Past Dalton researchers often disagree on the Bob and Emmett Dalton relationships with the Wesley Johnson family. Irregardless of just when and how their relationship began, Bob Dalton was known to have been in love with Lucy Johnson at the time their Coffeyville robbery plans were being made. Dalton lore suggests that Bob had planned to obtain sufficient funds from the Coffeyville banks to marry Lucy and to retire to a peaceful life. Emmett, who would marry Julia Johnson some fifteen years later, may also have had such thoughts. Neverthe-

The Wesley "Tex" Johnson home in Indian Territory

Julia and Lucy Johnson

less it has been determined that Bob, Grat, and Emmett Dalton camped along Onion Creek near the Wesley Johnson home the night before their raid on Coffeyville.

Their friends from ranch hand days, Bill Power and Dick "Tulsa Jack" Broadwell, joined the Daltons at their campsite to discuss final plans. Another friend, Harry Miller LeVan, who had been a neighbor during their years near Coffeyville, also joined them at their Onion Creek campsite. LeVan's father, John D. LeVan, was a cattleman and and money lender at the Condon Bank. His son, Harry, being somewhat estranged from his father, sympathized with the Daltons' plans but felt the plans the Daltons were making were foolish ones. LeVan did all he could to talk Bob Dalton out of such two bank robbery plans. Talking throughout the night, LeVan was unsuccessful in changing Bob Dalton's determination. Early on the morning of October 5, 1892, Bob, Grat, and Emmett Dalton, along with Bill Power, Dick Broadwell, and Harry Miller LeVan, rode toward Coffeyville from the west. The Daltons, realizing that they would be easily recognized by citizens in Coffeyville, attempted to disguise their appearance by wearing false beards. LeVan continued to plead with his friends until they reached the outskirts of Coffeyville. Realizing that his pleas were going unheard, he wished them luck and promised to keep his knowledge of the party a secret before leaving them.

A Coffeyville newspaper reporter, in his story about the Dalton raid the following day, mentioned that two parties had mentioned seeing six heavily armed and obviously disguised riders approaching

Coffeyville. These mentions of seeing six men when only five would be later accounted for has caused numerous theories over the years by Dalton writers as to the identity of this sixth man.

The most commonly reported theory mentions the outlaw Bill Doolin as being the sixth man. His horse becoming lame along their trail to Coffeyville, Doolin dropped out of the party. Another theory suggests that the sixth man may not have been a man, but rather Lucy Johnson, Bob's girl friend who chose to ride along with her lover. Some evidence as to this theory exists in the fact that one ladies glove was found tucked into his gunbelt when he was killed. Lucy supposedly left the party near the city limits of Coffeyville. Before leaving she gave Bob one of her gloves for good luck. She then rode to the Elmwood cemetery south of the city where she was to wait for Bob by Frank Dalton's grave. Other theories proclaim the sixth man as being Harry Miller LeVan, before he left the party. The sixth rider could have been Doolin, Johnson dressed in men's attire, or LeVan depending on at what point the two parties saw six riders along their trail into Coffeyville. The fact that Emmett Dalton refused to tell the identity of the sixth man for the rest of his life seems to indicate the sixth rider was Lucy Johnson, the sister of Emmett's wife Julia. Naturally Emmett would not have wanted to implicate a relative.

A few minutes after nine o'clock, five men reached the western city limits of Coffeyville and rode into the city at a slow trot on their fine horses. Each carried several weapons in their saddle bags and had Winchester rifles rolled in slickers tied behind their saddles.

Entering the city, the party rode into an alley behind the banks, dismounted and tied their horses. Walking toward Main Street a merchant noticed the false beards and apparent attempt to disguise themselves as the party walked by. The merchant then suspected that a bank robbery was being planned as he watched them enter the banks. Grat Dalton, Bill Power, and Dick Broadwell entered the Condon Bank while Bob and Emmett entered the First National across the street. Noting the men pulling their guns the merchant gave the alarm, "The banks are being robbed." By the time the Daltons had filled several bags with cash and began their escape, dozens of armed men had gathered in the street and a hail of bullets met the Daltons as they left the banks and ran toward the alley. City Marshall Charles T. Connelly killed Grat Dalton but as Dalton was falling he managed to fire a fatal bullet into the lawman. Bill Power was also one of the first to be brought down as he fought his way through the crowd.

Seeing Charles Connelly falling from Grat Dalton's gun, Coffeyville citizens Lucius Baldwin and George Cubine dashed to help their dying friend. Dick Broadwell then opened fire killing both Baldwin and Cubine. Broadwell made it to his horse although badly wounded with blood gushing from his mouth. Broadwell managed to flee the alley but his body was later found alongside the road some one mile out of town.

As Bob and Emmett Dalton went out the back door of the First National Bank they were met by Charles Brown. Bob shot him between the eyes.

The Condon Bank, Coffeyville, Kansas.
Courtesy Kansas State Historical Society.

The bodies of Bill Power, Grat Dalton, Dick Broadwell,
and Bob Dalton shortly after they were killed in Coffeyville
October 5, 1892. Courtesy Kansas State Historical Society.

Bob was mortally wounded by a barrage of gunfire as he ran down the alley and fell. Emmett reached his horse, turned and rode to where Bob had fallen and attempted to pull his brother onto his horse. Bob was then struck in the back by a deadly blow that ended his life. Emmett was shot some twenty-seven times before falling from his horse and being subdued by the citizens. Fifteen minutes after entering the banks, Bob Dalton, Grat Dalton, Bill Power, and Dick Broadwell had been killed and the badly wounded Emmett captured. Four brave Coffeyville citizens, Connelly, Baldwin, Cubine and Brown had also been killed while trying to protect their two banks.

Legend tells that Lucy Johnson, waiting for her lover Bob Dalton to pick her up in the Elmwood cemetery as the gang was to flee south, rode into the city after hearing the raging gun battle. Noting her beloved Bob's body on the street, she turned and rode eastward into Arkansas to never be heard of again.

Emmett, the only survivor of the Coffeyville affair, somehow miraculously survived his many wounds, was tried, and given a life sentence in the Kansas State Prison. The bodies of Grat and Bob Dalton were claimed by the Dalton family and buried in Coffeyville's Elmwood cemetery.

Newspaper editor D. Stewart Elliott wrote in his lengthy article about the Daltons' raid that he had interviewed J. M. and J. L. Seldonridge and Mr. and Mrs. Hollingsworth who had been traveling west of the city and noticed the Dalton party as they were riding toward Coffeyville. Both parties were clear in their statements about noticing six riders.

Since only five were brought down in Coffeyville, the mystery as to the identity of the sixth man seen with the Dalton party has created numerous theories over the years. Since Bill Doolin was known to have been with the Daltons during their Adair train robbery, the theory that Bill Doolin was the sixth rider emerged. Emmett Dalton was never known to reveal the identity of such another party being with them. This fact suggests that such a sixth man may have been their good friend Harry Miller LeVan whose father was a money lender in the Condon Bank. Naturally Emmett would not have wanted to implicate such a friend. Also the evidence previously presented about Lucy Johnson dressed in men's attire accompanying the party to the outskirts of Coffeyville has merit. Emmett would not have wanted to implicate the Johnson family in having part in the affair in any way. It is also possible that the group may have originally consisted of eight and depending on what point each dropped out along the route, Doolin, LeVan, or Johnson could have been the sixth man reported seen.

Although records indicate that Emmett had courted Julia for several years before the Coffeyville raid, she had chosen to marry a half-breed Cherokee, Robert Gilstrap, in January of 1887. Their daughter Jennie was born in November of that same year. This was to be a short union, however, as Gilstrap was killed in a shooting argument with Frank Leno in Bartle's store on Christmas Eve of 1889. Julia may then have once again turned her attentions to Emmett Dalton. She helped them escape a posse after their Adair train robbery in 1892 and visited the badly wounded Emmett in

Coffeyville often before he was sent to prison. Julia took as her second husband in 1902 Earnest Lewis. Lewis reportedly had killed men in the states of Washington and Colorado and in the Chickasaw Nation. He also illegally sold liquor in Indian Territory. Deputy Marshalls Fred Keeler and George Williams were attempting to arrest Lewis for his illegal liquor sales activities during the celebration of Oklahoma statehood on November 16, 1907. Lewis and Williams were both killed in the shootout that occurred.

Resulting from Emmett Dalton being a model prisoner and from the help his old friend Harry Miller LeVan gave him, Emmett was pardoned in the spring of 1907. He then went to Tulsa where he became a security officer and opened a butcher shop business with Scout Younger. He renewed his old relationship with Julia Johnson Lewis soon afterward and they married on September 1, 1908 in Bartlesville. They remained in Bartlesville for a short while. While there they adopted a son which they referred to as Bill Dalton. Little is know of this boy.

They moved to Los Angeles a short time later. There Emmett, being somewhat of a celebrity, became involved in the film industry. He helped produce and appeared in the film "When the Daltons Rode." Emmett, with the help of ghost writers, wrote two books about the Dalton Gang, invested in real estate, and became a building contractor. In 1924 Emmett returned to Coffeyville for a special homecoming celebration. While there he arranged to purchase a monument for the grave of his brothers.

The wounds Emmett received during the raid

Emmett Dalton

Julia Johnson Dalton

on Coffeyville never healed properly and plagued him all of his life. He developed diabetes and suffered his first stroke some eight years before his death. He died from a second stroke at age sixty-six on July 13, 1937. His body was cremated. Emmett's sister in Kingfisher, Oklahoma contacted Alva D. Mauk, a Kingfisher undertaker for assistance in getting Emmett's ashes returned to Kingfisher for burial without creating publicity and a problem for her. Mauk contacted the Los Angeles funeral home and arranged for the ashes to be shipped to him. On arrival by train, Leona and Mauk waited until after dark, then they took a post hole digger to the Kingfisher cemetery and buried Emmett's remains.

Julia married a John R. Johnson after her husband's death. She died on May 20, 1943 and was also cremated. Her ashes were returned for burial in the Dewey, Oklahoma cemetery.

Bill Dalton, having lost considerable respect in California as a result of his brothers' activities, for some reason returned to Indian Territory. Apparently forsaking his wife Jane and their two children Charles and Gracie Dalton, Bill teamed up with the noted outlaw Bill Doolin to form what became known as the Dalton-Doolin Gang. Accused of robbing a bank in Longview, Texas, Bill Dalton was cornered by a posse led by Texas lawman Loss Hart and killed near the Elk community on June 6, 1894. His wife and brother Ben traveled to Ardmore to claim his body which Jane returned to California for burial in the Blevin family plot in Turlock Memorial Park in Turlock, California.

Ben Dalton became mentally disturbed and spent his last years at the Western State Hospital in Fort Supply, Oklahoma. He died there March 16, 1936. Littleton Dalton died in California. Simon, the youngest Dalton brother, was killed in a train-automobile accident in 1927. Adeline, the matriarch of the Dalton clan died at her Kingfisher home January 24, 1925. The Daltons' sister Eva Mae married John N. Whipple. She died in Kingfisher on January 27, 1939. Leona Dalton, the last survivor of the James Lewis Dalton, Jr. and Adeline Dalton family never married and died in Kingfisher April 18, 1964.

Had Bob, Grat, and Emmett Dalton not attempted to rob two banks simultaneously in Coffeyville, Kansas on October 5, 1892, it is doubtful the Dalton name would have been significant in the history of the American West. That bold attempt earned the Daltons national notoriety and the fact Coffeyville's brave citizens rose up to prevent such criminal activity within their town helped encourage other cities to bring law and order necessary to the settlement of the west.

John Wesley Hardin

Chapter 3

John Wesley Hardin

John Wesley Hardin, sometimes referred to as the Texas Jesse James, was one of the most intriguing and complicated personalities in the annals of western history and folklore. Not only did he develop a reputation as a notorious gunfighter throughout the southwest, with over twenty-one deaths credited to his lightening speed with a gun when provoked, he also became a lawyer and was considered a good citizen and community leader in El Paso. The fact that Hardin was killed by a bullet in the back of the head, like Jesse James, Belle Starr, Wild Bill Hickok, and others, perhaps further elevated him to the ranks of folk heroes and heroines in Old West literature. Following the pattern, pulp novel writers further promoted Hardin as a gunfighter not to be taken lightly. True facts of Hardin's real personality, like that of many others, have therefore been clouded with folklore.

Born in Bonham, Texas on May 26, 1853, John Wesley Hardin was the second son of the Reverend J. G. Hardin, a Methodist minister, and his wife Elizabeth.

Hardin was named after the noted leader John Wesley, of England, who helped form the Methodist denomination. Although Rev. Hardin was a minister, he and his family were strong supporters of the Confederate cause during the Civil War and despised all Negroes. Hardin wrote his memoirs while in prison and mentioned that he first got in trouble when he killed a Negro bully that came after him with a club when he was only fifteen years of age. He killed the black youth with his father's old Colt pistol. Hardin's personality and the direction he took in life can be traced to those deep family feelings over the defeat of the Confederacy. Hardin necessarily had to leave his education at an early age as a result of the killing of the black youth. Hardin mentioned these problems in his memoirs, saying "But from the injustice and misrule of the people who had subjugated the South, I had to leave my family."

Hardin then made his way to Navarro County after shooting down three Union soldiers who were pursuing him for the killing of the black youth. There he became a ranch hand. The extreme tension that still prevailed following the Civil War somehow contributed to Hardin's next gunfight. Along with a cousin, Simp Dixon, they killed two more Union soldiers. A short time later Hardin became irate over a Jim Bradley's accusation that Hardin was cheating in a saloon poker game. Both stood up from the table simultaneously and drew their weapons. Hardin's speed resulted in Bradley's death. This quickness with a gun was developed by Hardin not only by his many hours of practice while still a youth; but also, the unusual method he had in carrying his weapons contributed. Hardin had two holsters sewn into his vest which allowed his guns to point inward across his chest. Crossing his arms in a wide arch in a single motion saved valuable seconds over reaching for guns on the hip.

Next Hardin was reported to have killed a circus roustabout in some type of quarrel. While in Kosse, Texas with a dance hall girl, he killed a man who tried to rob him. Though most of his killings to this point had been in self defense, Hardin nevertheless became a highly wanted man. He was arrested by law authorities in Longview, Texas for a murder blamed on him in which he emphatically denied having a part. While being jailed in Longview, Hardin somehow purchased a Colt revolver from another prisoner. While being taken to Waco, Texas to stand trial for the murder Hardin insisted he did not commit, Hardin killed his guard and escaped. Three Yankee soldiers were sent out to recapture the youth. All three soldiers were slain on the open prairie.

Hardin then made his way to a large cattle ranch owned by William C. Cohron, where he was employed as a ranch hand. Cohron was killed by a cattle rustler named Juan Bideno a short time after Hardin arrived at the ranch. With another ranch hand, Hugh Anderson, Hardin tracked Bideno for several weeks. Finally locating him, Hardin was credited with shooting the bandit in the heart in August of 1871.

James Butler "Wild Bill" Hickok, another personality whose life was ended from a shot to the back of his head, and one chosen as the leading character in novelists' portrayals of the west, was serving as the town marshall in Abilene, Texas in 1871. Abilene was a wide open cattle town with violent gun battles taking place daily around this frontier city. Hardin rode into Abilene with a few of his ranch hand friends and, after spending several hours in a saloon, Hardin ran into the streets shooting his revolvers wildly into the air. Hickok approached Hardin and demanded his guns. Apparently aware of Hickok's reputation with a gun, Hardin pretended to be handing his guns to him and in a quick move reversed his weapons to point toward Hickok. Although intoxicated, Hardin knew better than to shoot the famous marshall and simply informed Hickok that he planned to remain in town and would be peaceful. Hickok, perhaps also aware of Hardin's reputation, backed down and left Hardin only with a warning. This bit of Hardin history reported by John Wesley in his memoirs is considered by historians to be fiction. Irregardless of what the true events taking place between Hardin and Hickok were that day, Hickok did not arrest Hardin and Hardin remained in the city for several weeks thereafter. Hardin apparently stayed out of trouble for several weeks until one night a ruffian in a saloon was loudly proclaiming his hatred for yellow Texans. Hardin shot down the belligerent cowboy. Fearing Hickok, with whom he almost was brought to a test, Hardin quickly left town.

Hardin next took a ranch hand job in Gonzales County. There two Negro policemen, John Lackey and Green Paramoor learned Hardin was there and went hunting for him. Hardin shot Paramoor and ran Lackey out of the county after wounding him several times.

Hardin again faced trouble while gambling in a Trinty City saloon in 1872. Phil Sublet shot Hardin with a load of buckshot over a gambling quarrel. A posse searching for Hardin over the Paramoor killing shortly thereafter rode into town and almost captured the elusive Hardin. After a furious gun battle in the streets Hardin once again escaped. Hardin was wounded badly in the leg during this battle with the posse. Apparently in pain from the wounds received in Trinty City, and no doubt tired by now of constantly being involved in one gun fight after another, Hardin decided to surrender. He rode to the Gonzales county jail and handed over his guns to sheriff Richard Reagan.

Hardin had married Jane Bowen in 1872. Now, though only nineteen years of age with some eighteen deaths credited to him, Hardin apparently began to mellow. Hoping to somehow escape imprisonment by claiming self defense in most of the crimes charged to him, he yearned for a peaceful life as a rancher with his new bride. Confinement behind bars for several weeks finally eroded such dreams for the free spirited Hardin. Sawing his way through the jail cell with a saw smuggled to him by a friend, Hardin once again escaped to the Texas prairie. Hardin then sought refuge with his relatives in the Taylor family of DeWitt County, Texas. A family feud that dated back to the Civil War between the Taylor and Sutton families was still a heated one when Hardin arrived. The Suttons were controlling the territory with an army of some two hundred ranch hands. Backing the Sutton faction were Abel "Shanghai" Pierce, a cattle baron in the region; Jack Helm, a lawman; and Joe Tumilson. Hardin overheard a sheriff, J. B. Morgan, making bad comments about him near Cureo, Texas. The proud Hardin's explosive speed with his guns resulted in Morgan's instant death from a bullet to Morgan's left eye. Hardin then had to leave town again.

The Taylor-Sutton war would continue to rage on through 1873. After several Taylor supporters had been killed, Jim Taylor swore vengeance on old Bill Sutton, the leader of the family. Once again calling in his gunfighter cousin, Hardin, an ambush was planned for the Banks Saloon. When Sutton entered with some of his boys, gunfire broke out. Barely escaping with minor wounds, Sutton was lucky to have survived. A few weeks later Hardin killed Jake Chrisman and Jim Cox who had been with Sutton at the Banks Saloon gunfight. Soon afterward lawman Jack Helm was killed by Hardin as Helm attempted to knife Jim Taylor in a blacksmith shop. The Taylor-Sutton war continued into 1874 and finally came to an end when Hardin assisted his relatives Jim and Bill Taylor in surrounding Bill Sutton and his chief supporter Gabe Slaughter as they were attempting to board a New Orleans bound steamer at Indianola. Jim Taylor ended his pledge of vengeance by sending a bullet through Sutton's heart as Bill Taylor simultaneously killed Slaughter. Finally the decades-old Sutton-Taylor war came to an end. Hardin then returned to his wife in Comanche, Texas.

Although John Wesley Hardin was now a highly wanted man with rewards posted for his arrest throughout the southwest, Hardin felt relatively safe in Comanche. Most of the citizens there, including Comanche Sheriff John Karnes, had admired the Taylor family and respected Hardin for his brave assistance to the family in bringing down the Sutton faction. There Hardin enjoyed playing cards in the local saloons and making friends with most of the town's citizens. Although only twenty-one years of age, Hardin had already become a legend with whom the citizens of Comanche were proud to associate. The town held a celebration and horse races in Hardin's honor in which Hardin won more than $3,000.

Such attention and acclaim Hardin was

receiving no doubt provided John Wesley with a sense of freedom and protection that made him forget he was still a highly wanted man for the now dozens of deaths brought forth by his two Colts. During the celebration Sheriff Charlie Webb rode into town. Seeing Hardin on the streets, Webb walked toward him. Noting his approach, Hardin questioned him. After stating that he had no papers for his arrest, Hardin invited the sheriff into a saloon for a drink. Hardin led the way toward the saloon door. Bud Dixon noted the sheriff reaching for his gun as Hardin turned his back, and Dixon yelled a warning to Hardin. Hardin quickly turned, drawing his weapons with his usual speed. Hardin's bullet struck Sheriff Brown in the cheek, killing him instantly. Brown's gun fired as he fell and wounded Hardin in the side. The killing of Sheriff Brown forced Hardin to bid his family and friends farewell and run again. A lynch mob found Hardin's brother Joe and hanged him. His friends Tom and Bud Dixon were also hanged. Ham Anderson and Alex Barrickman were hunted down and shot for also having been friends of Hardin's. The reward for Hardin's arrest had now grown to $4,000.

The Pinkerton Detective Agency, the Texas Rangers, as well as dozens of bounty hunters all began searching for the elusive Hardin. Months went by with continuing reports of Hardin being seen in Georgia, Florida, Louisiana, Alabama and other locations.

After some three years the Texas Rangers determined that Hardin was in the Pensacola, Florida region when they intercepted a letter Hardin had written to his wife. On August 23, 1877 a large

John Wesley Hardin

posse of Rangers waited at the Pensacola train station suspecting Hardin to be boarding a train. As he was spotted boarding, groups of lawmen entered on both ends of Hardin's passenger car. Ranger Lieutenant John B. Armstrong walked to Hardin and held his pistol to Hardin's forehead. One of Hardin's companions pulled his gun and fired at Armstrong, the bullet going through his hat. Armstrong then took careful aim and shot the man in the chest. Hardin caught his two vest pistols in his suspenders preventing him from drawing. Armstrong then hit Hardin in the head, knocking him unconscious.

Insisting that he was not Hardin, he claimed to be J. H. Swain all the way back to Texas; but, by the time the party crossed the Texas border, finally admitted that he was John Wesley Hardin. First taken to jail in Austin, the Gonzales courthouse was packed with spectators in September, 1877 when Hardin was taken there to be tried for the murder of Sheriff Webb.

Pleading his own defense, the eloquent Hardin swore that the only men he had ever killed had been killed in self defense. He further claimed that he knew Sheriff Webb had come to Comanche to kill him and not to arrest him. He called on the jurors to look at the fact his father and family were good people and that his innocent brother had been lynched. Hardin claimed he had no choice but to draw and fire when Sheriff Webb pulled his gun.

Hardin's Shakespearean eloquence had swayed the jury and, rather than being found guilty and sentenced to hang, the jury found it to be second degree murder. Hardin was then sentenced to twenty-one years at hard labor in the Rusk Prison in Huntsville, Texas.

Hardin served sixteen years. Claiming to be a reformed man, he was released on March 16, 1894. Hardin was age forty at the time of his release. Hardin had begun studying law while in prison. His wife, Jane Bowen, had died November 6, 1892. Upon his release, Hardin took his children — Mary Elizabeth (Mollie), who was born February 6, 1873; John Wesley, born August 3, 1875; and Callie (also called Jane), born July 15, 1877 — to Gonzales, where he lived with an old friend, Fred Duderstadt, on his ranch. There he worked as a cowhand and continued his law studies. Finishing his law studies, and obtaining a license to practice, he first set up a law office in Junction, Texas. Soon afterward he moved to the booming border town of El Paso where the *El Paso Times* newspaper heralded Hardin's rehabilitation, good citizenship, and leadership in the community.

It wasn't long, however, until Hardin's restless spirit once again found him frequenting the El Paso saloon and gambling halls. Soon he met and took as a second wife Callie Lewis in El Paso.

Callie was only eighteen years of age at the time and soon grew tired of Hardin's carousing and divorced him. Hardin then began to drink heavily and was often found passed out in numerous saloons and dives around El Paso.

Hardin became enamored with a married lady who was the known wife of the outlaw cattle rustler Martin McRose. Seen together often around El Paso for several weeks, McRose got into some type of heated argument with saloon girls one evening and was arrested and jailed by an El Paso lawman named John Selman. Hardin then began making bad remarks about Selman's heritage and unethical practices as a lawman and often stated, "Old John had better go fixed at all times." In other words, Hardin made it known that Selman could expect to face Hardin's guns in the future.

Upon hearing Hardin's threat, John Selman strapped on his gun and walked to the Acme saloon on the night of August 19, 1895. Selman noted Hardin sitting at the bar playing dice with the bartender. Hardin saw Selman in the mirror with his gun pointed at Hardin's back, and he started to turn when Selman fired. The bullet split open the back of Hardin's head and he died instantly. Although highly ridiculed by the public for shooting the now folk hero Hardin in the back, Selman's attorney, Albert Fall, convinced a jury that Hardin was reaching for his vest guns at the time. Convinced Selman's actions were in self-defense, Selman was acquitted.

Chapter 4

Gunfight at the O.K. Corral

Wyatt Berry Stapp Earp

Few peace officers or gunfighters in the annals of Old West history can equal the notoriety gained by Wyatt Berry Stapp Earp. Born near Monmouth, Illinois on March 19, 1848, his life would be of little significance and he certainly would not have earned a place in the history of Old West had it not been for the encounter Wyatt, his brothers Virgil and Morgan Earp, and a consumptive dentist, John "Doc" Holliday, had with the Clantons and McLowerys near the O.K. Corral in Tombstone, Arizona on October 26, 1881. Some historians consider this controversial gunfight with outlaw cowboys to be murder of the worst sort, while others place the event in history as being a most significant example of western lawmen's dedication to bringing law and order to the West. Irregardless of these historical debates, Wyatt Earp, his brothers, and Doc Holliday were catapulted into the realm of heroism during a 30 second blaze of bullets near Fly's Photography Shop and the O.K. Corral on that fateful day.

Wyatt Earp left Illinois with his family in his late teens and settled on a farm near Lamar, Missouri. There he met and married his first wife, Vrilla Sutherland, on January 10, 1870. The ceremony was performed by his father, N. P. Earp, who was a Justice of the Peace. His wife died along with the infant in childbirth less than a year later. Wyatt's first job as a law officer was that of Lamar's town marshall when he was age twenty-three. Shortly after his election to the job, his wife died and Wyatt got into a serious quarrel with his wife's brothers and decided to leave Lamar. Wyatt found government surveyors in Springfield, Missouri and was employed by them as a hunter to provide meat for the survey crews. Leaving for Baxter Springs, Kansas in 1870, Wyatt took his hunting party south into the Indian Territory of what is now Oklahoma. There they hunted throughout the Creek and Choctaw Nations before rambling back north to Arkansas City, Kansas where they were paid by the government for their services in 1871.

It was during this Indian Territory hunting expedition period that Earp was accused of horse theft. Fort Smith, Arkansas Federal Court records indicate that a grand jury found Wyatt S. Earp, Edward Kennedy, and John Shown guilty of stealing six horses from James Keys in Indian Territory on March 28, 1871. U. S. Deputy Marshall J. G. Owens reported on April 6, 1871 that he had arrested the three men. Court records are, from this point, unclear. It appears that Earp and possibly also Shown were the only two who could post the $500 bail. Only Kennedy was tried and acquitted. Earp and Shown apparently never returned to Fort Smith for trial.

After being paid in Arkansas City, Kansas, Wyatt left for Kansas City to prepare for a buffalo hunting trip along with brothers Virgil, Morgan, and James. At age twenty-five Wyatt became city marshall for the trail town of Ellsworth, Kansas on August 18, 1873. A year later he became marshall in the even tougher trail town of Wichita. After innumerable encounters with drunken cowhands, gunfighters, and gamblers around Wichita, Wyatt had earned a good reputation as a lawman. By 1876 his reputation as a "town tamer" earned him the marshall's job in Dodge City, Kansas. There Wyatt

John Henry "Doc" Holliday

first met and became good friends with Doc Holliday, Batt Masterson, Bill Tilghman and others who also would earn a rightful place in the history of the early West.

Doc Holliday was born in Georgia in 1852. The son of a Confederate major who had been killed in the Civil War, Holliday received training in dentistry at Biltmore College. While in college he contracted tuberculosis and was told he had a maximum of four years to live. Embittered over his fate, Holliday vented his fury upon four young Negro boys who were trespassing in his favorite swimming hole. Despising Negroes and embittered over his father's death, the loss of the Confederate cause, and his illness, Holliday killed two of the Negroes with a shotgun and badly wounded the two others. Full of hatred, he left Georgia for the young city of Dallas where he first opened up an office for dentistry in a climate he hoped would be better for his condition. Holliday seldom practiced his trade, however, as he soon found his natural skill as a gambler in the local saloons to be more profitable and rewarding. Holliday fled to Jacksboro, Texas, a thriving town for gamblers near Fort Richardson, after killing a wealthy rancher who accused Holliday of cheating. Another gambling altercation with a soldier there forced Holliday to leave hurriedly with a posse on his trail. Soon afterward the posse abandoned the chase. Holliday then settled in Denver where he not only found further relief for his tuberculosis but also a gambler's paradise in Denver saloons. Once again Holliday was in a fight over a saloon card game with Bud Ryan. Holiday seriously wounded Ryan with a bowie knife and fled for Fort Griffin,

Texas. There Holliday met Kate Fisher. Known to history as Big Nose Kate, they were to remain lovers throughout their lives. Kate saved Holliday from a necktie party after Holliday killed Ed Bailey at Fort Griffin. Escaping to Dodge City, the desperate Holliday and Wyatt Earp met and developed a loyal friendship that was to remain with them throughout their lifetime.

In Dodge City, Earp and his friend Holliday not only were unusually effective in maintaining law and order but also used their positions to profit from gambling, prostitution, and saloon business enterprises.

Silver strikes in Tombstone, Arizona had not only attracted some 12,000 wealth seekers to the city, but also created a need for the lawman services the Earps could offer and gambling opportunities for the now even more desperate and alcoholic Doc Holliday. Wyatt, Virgil, and Morgan Earp, along with Doc Holliday left Dodge City for Tombstone in 1879. Holliday took along his devoted common-law wife, Big Nose Kate.

Wyatt first took a job as a Wells Fargo guard. Later he became a deputy sheriff for Pima County. When Cochise County was formed, Wyatt's rival John Behan, who was supported by the ranchers of the territory, was chosen as sheriff. Earp then consoled himself with playing poker in the Club Oriental and assisting brother Virgil who had first become assistant marshall and the following June was appointed marshall for the city of Tombstone.

The Earps' friend Doc Holliday was suspected of being involved in the robbery of a stagecoach that left Tombstone on the night of March 15, 1881.

Virgil Earp

Morgan Earp

Three of the four masked men who robbed the coach were identified later by a man who had tended the robbers' horses as being Bill Leonard, Jim Crane, and Harry Head. Passengers reported that the fourth robber, who had fired the shot killing the stage driver Bud Philpot, was a small, frail man fitting the description of Doc Holliday. Marshall Earp dismissed the suspicion of Holliday as being ludicrous and accused a group of cowboy outlaw ruffians and the Clanton gang of cattle rustlers of being involved with the robbery and murder of Philpot. N. H. Clanton, referred to around town as "Old Man" Clanton, his three sons, John Ringo, Curly Bill Brocius, Tom and Frank McLowery, Frank Stillwell, and others who were well-known cattle rustlers of the region had become arch enemies of the Earps. Protected by the county sheriff John Behan, the Earps' open remarks about some day putting a stop to the Clanton gang's widespread rustling activities had continually contributed to the feud between the Earps and the cowboy outlaws known as the Clanton gang. The stagecoach robbery and Bud Philpot's death further intensified the Earp-Clanton feud when the Earps openly accused the Clanton gang of participating in the affair.

Young Ike Clanton, openly ignoring the Earps' self-imposed city ordinance banning firearms in the city, rode into town on October 25 with his brother Billy Clanton and Tom and Frank McLowery. Wyatt Earp openly challenged the Clantons to go for their guns in a saloon after midnight but the young cowboys refused and left.

Learning that the Clanton and McLowery brothers were in town and armed, Marshall Virgil

Ike Clanton   *Newman "Old Man" Clanton*

Tom McLowery

Robert McLowery

Earp expected trouble. He appointed not only his brother Morgan, but also brother Wyatt and their friend Doc Holliday as deputies. The night passed without any further disturbance. At sunrise Marshall Virgil Earp went home for rest. A short time later Morgan Earp went to Virgil's house to inform him that Ike Clanton was threatening to kill Virgil on sight. The brothers then walked to town where they encountered Clanton wearing a revolver on his hip and carrying a Winchester rifle. Marshall Earp walked up to Clanton, grabbed the rifle, hit him in the head with the rifle butt, and took his pistol. He then marched Clanton to the police court where he entered a complaint against Clanton for carrying weapons. Clanton was fined $27.50 by the court around one o'clock. Released upon his promise to leave town, the Earps returned to the sheriff's office.

Around 2:30 p.m. R. F. Coleman came to Marshall Earp's office where he informed him of seeing Ike and Billy Clanton and the two McLowery brothers, all heavily armed, in heavy conversation in Dunbar's Corral. Coleman, suspecting trouble, first went to Sheriff Behan's office. Behan, being a friend of the Clantons, left immediately to disarm the Clantons and to attempt to get them out of town.

Virgil, Morgan, Wyatt and Doc Holliday then checked their weapons and began walking toward the Clantons' location near Fly's Photography Gallery. Sheriff Behan, who had been unsuccessful in disarming the Clantons and McLowerys, met the Earps in the middle of the street and attempted to stop them. Brushing Behan aside, the four men continued in a slow place toward the O.K. Corral.

As they approached, Virgil Earp told the party, "Give up your weapons and throw up your arms." At the same instant two shots were fired simultaneously by Doc Holliday and Frank McLowery. The Clanton-Earp feud had reached the explosion stage and within the next thirty seconds some thirty shots were fired. Tom McLowery fell first but raised and fired again as he fell. Billy Clanton fell next. Mr. Fly, owner of Fly's Photography Gallery had been observing the affair and when Billy Clanton attempted to raise and fire again, Fly ran to where Clanton lay and took his pistol from him. Ike Clanton, whose arms had been taken from him earlier in the day at police court, was unarmed. When the firing began, he ran to Allen Street where refuge was taken in a dance hall. Frank McLowery attempted to run but fell a few yards away mortally wounded. Morgan Earp was shot and fell. Doc Holliday was hit in the left hip but remained standing and continued to fire rapidly. Virgil Earp was wounded in the leg. He staggered but kept firing. Wyatt stood and fired in rapid succession. He was not wounded.

As the firing subsided, Sheriff Behan walked up to Wyatt and stated, "I'll have to arrest you." Wyatt calmly answered, "I won't be arrested today. I am right here and plan to stay. You have deceived us. You said these men were not armed."

Tom and Frank McLowery and Billy Clanton all died within a few minutes after being shot. Marshall Virgil Earp had been shot in the calf of his right leg. Morgan Earp had been shot in the right shoulder. Doc Holliday's wound in the hip was minor since the scabbard for his pistol had broken the bullet's force. Wyatt was not wounded.

Dr. Matthews impanelled a coroner's jury to view the bodies after they were laid in a cabin at the rear of Dunbar's stables on Fifth Street.

The *Tombstone Epitaph* reported in coverage of the event the next day that Marshall Earp was entirely justified in his efforts to disarm these men. The Earps also were justified in defending themselves which they did most bravely. The newspaper further reported that the Earps have the full support of all of the city's good citizens. "If the present lesson is not sufficient to teach the cowboy element that they cannot come into the streets of Tombstone, armed with six-shooters and Henry rifles to hunt down their victims, then citizens will take such steps necessary to preserve the peace and forever bar such further raids."

Irregardless of the *Epitaph's* sympathy with the Earps, warrants were sworn out for their arrest on a charge for murder and a hearing was held before Justice of the Peace Wells Spicer. The hearing lasted for thirty days. After numerous witnesses testified, Justice Spicer's opinion was that the Earps acted in self-defense. Spicer did state however that Virgil Earp committed an injudicious and censurable act by calling upon Wyatt Earp and J. H. Holliday to assist him in arresting and disarming the Clantons and McLowerys. Since Morgan Earp had often served his brother Virgil as a deputy, he was not mentioned by Justice Spicer.

The funeral for Billy Clanton and Tom and Frank McLowery was the largest ever witnessed in Tombstone. Their bodies were neatly dressed and placed in handsome caskets with heavy silver trimming. Each had an engraved silver plate bearing his name, place of birth, and date of death: William H. Clanton, 19 years of age, a native of Texas; Thomas McLowery, 25 years of age, and Frank McLowery, 29 years of age, natives of Mississippi. A short time before burial, photographs were taken of the dead.

Ike Clanton, who had been unarmed and fled from the O.K. Corral when the shooting started, was suspected of planning revenge against the Earps. Around 11:30 p.m. on Wednesday, December 28, 1881, Virgil Earp was fired upon by several men as he left the Oriental Saloon. Carried to a hotel, a doctor examined him to find several buckshot wounds in his left side, back, and arm.

On March 18, 1882 Morgan Earp was playing billiards with Bob Hatch in Campbell and Hatch's Billiard Parlor. A group of men, including Wyatt, were watching. Around 10:50 p.m. a group of men crept up to the rear door of the pool hall and fired two shots into the room. One slug entered Morgan's stomach and shattered his spinal column. The second shot barely missed Wyatt as he ran to his brother. Morgan died less than an hour afterward. Once again, associates of the Clanton gang were suspected of the crime.

Two days later, on March 20, Wyatt, his younger brother Warren, Sherman McMasters, Doc Holliday, and Turkey Creek Jack Johnson all accompanied Virgil Earp and his wife to Tucson. There Virgil planned to take Morgan's body to Colton, California by train and to convalesce for a period with his parents.

Frank Stillwell and Ike Clanton were waiting

for the party at the depot. Stillwell, who had been the chief suspect in Morgan's murder, was run down and killed by the Earp party. Ike Clanton escaped.

Virgil left for California where he later died of natural causes. Wyatt Earp, his brother Warren Earp, Doc Holliday, Sherman McMasters, and "Turkey Creek" Jack Johnson left Arizona in the spring of 1882. Arriving in Colorado they each went their separate ways. Wyatt spent most of his time around the cities of Gunnison and Lake City where he was involved in a shooting in September of 1884 and was wounded in the arm.

During the winter of 1883-1884 Wyatt and his wife Josephine went to the mining town of Coer d'Alene, Idaho. Wyatt managed a saloon there for several months. By way of Texas, Wyatt moved to San Diego, California in 1885 and by 1896 was found living in San Francisco. In December of 1896 Wyatt, being still popular for his O.K. Corral gunfight participation, helped promote and referee the championship fight between Bob Fitzsimmions and Jack Sharkey.

During the height of the Klondike gold rush, Wyatt traveled with his wife to Alaska. There he built and operated the Dexter saloon in Nome. From there Wyatt went to Toopah, Nevada to manage still another saloon for a brief period then drifted throughout the desserts of Arizona and California prospecting and gambling. Wyatt died of natural causes at age eighty on January 13, 1929.

Doc Holliday continued to seek out climate advantages and fertile gambling towns until his tuberculosis and alcoholism overcame him. He died in Glenwood Springs, Colorado in a sanitarium at age thirty-five.

Certainly the reputations bestowed upon the Earps and their sickly associate Doc Holliday would not have been created had their brief gunfight at the O.K. Corral not occurred. The subject of hundreds of books, articles, and films over the years, what may have been only an insignificant event in the history of the West became a major subject of discussion for those who enjoy western history and created folk heroism as gunfighters for the Earps and Doc Holliday.

Author Phillip Steele, left, and Fort Smith, Arkansas Mayor Bill Vines with Flossie Mae Wiley, great-great granddaughter of Belle Starr.

Belle Starr

Chapter 5

Belle Starr

Myra Maebelle Shirley, Belle Starr

John Shirley, born in Virginia in 1794, moved to Kentucky at an early age where he became a very successful breeder of fine Kentucky horses. There he met and married Elizabeth Pennington in 1837. John, his wife and son Preston Shirley, from a previous marriage, left Kentucky a few years before the Civil War and settled lands west of Carthage, Missouri near the Georgia City and Medoc communities. There, Judge Shirley, as he was called, built a home and stables for his Kentucky horses. He also developed a race track there and continued to breed and race his fine Kentucky horses. A few years after his arrival in Missouri, he acquired a hotel and tavern in Carthage which he named The Shirley House. Judge Shirley then moved his family to The Shirley House, leaving several slaves that had come with them from Kentucky to manage his horse ranch. Fine food and a popular tavern made The Shirley House a favorite meeting place in southwestern Missouri where heated discussions relating to politics and the impending Civil War were held.

Other than Judge Shirley's son Preston, all of his children were born on their Missouri horse ranch. Charlotte was born in 1838; John Allison, referred to as Bud, in 1842; Myra Maebelle on February 5, 1848; Edwin Benton in 1850; Mansfield in 1852, and Cravens in 1858.

The Shirleys, being quite prominent in the region, saw to it that all their children were educated well. Myra Maebelle, whom they called Mae and later Belle, was instructed in music and all of the social etiquette of the day. Being quite talented on the piano, young Maebelle often entertained in her father's tavern where she was first exposed to the strongly debated politics that developed during the period prior to the Civil War. The Shirleys were slave owners and strongly supported the Confederate cause as did most southern Missouri citizens. The Shirley House became a popular meeting place for those who supported the Confederacy. Indications are that it was first at their popular tavern that the Shirley family may have become acquainted with many young Missouri farm boys who would later serve with Quantrill guerrilla forces during the Civil War.

As the war began, John Allison "Bud" Shirley enlisted. During this period, young Belle was known to have dressed in men's attire and regularly carried messages to Confederate camps regarding Federal movements she overheard at The Shirley House. Bud Shirley was killed in a skirmish near Sarcoxie, Missouri in 1864. Belle and her mother then went to pick up the body of their beloved brother and son. Before leaving with the body, Belle told the remaining Confederates in the region that she would marry the man who would run down and kill the man who had killed her brother.

Shortly before the city of Carthage was burned by Union forces, John Shirley took his family to Scyene, Texas, east of Dallas, to protect his family from the ravages of the war. In Scyene, Shirley once again established a tavern and boarding house. Belle helped support the family by taking jobs as a piano player in nearby Dallas. Because she often rode home late at night, she began wearing two pearl handled pistols for protection, over her long velvet dresses. The appearance of a female riding side-saddle along Dallas streets, dressed in stylish velvet and wearing pistols no doubt contributed to Belle's popularity at an early age.

As the Civil War was drawing to a close, old Missouri friends and remnants of Quantrill guerrilla bands drifted into Texas. Jesse James, Cole Younger, Jim Reed, Bloody Bill Anderson, and others who later rode with outlaw bands often stopped by their friend John Shirley's tavern. On one such occasion, Belle Shirley, although only eighteen years of age, rode off with a party of such men she admired to Collin County, Texas. There on November 1, 1866, Belle was coerced into marrying James C. Reed in a horseback ceremony directed by a justice of the peace. Legend explains this quick marriage as Belle's decision to keep the promise she made to marry the man who killed the man who had killed her beloved brother Bud Shirley in Missouri.

John Shirley strongly objected to his daughter marrying the outlaw Reed and attempted to have the marriage nullified and keep them apart. He took Belle to his son Preston's farm in Palo Pinto County, Texas where Belle was to be kept from Reed. Reed soon found her, however, and took his wife to stay with his family in Rich Hill, Missouri. Their first child, Rose Pearl Reed, was born there in 1868.

Reed became a wanted man as a result of his activities with various outlaw gangs during this period. Belle then returned to Scyene with her child. From 1868 to 1870 Belle Reed not only became a popular Dallas saloon entertainer, but also became a partner with a Dallas business man in a livery stable in Dallas. During this time Belle

*Belle Shirley and Jim Reed, wedding picture 1867.
Courtesy Charles Reed Young.*

provided a ready market for stolen horses her husband Jim Reed and the Starr gang in Indian Territory regularly brought to her.

Jim Reed was already a wanted man with a sizeable reward for his capture when he became involved with the Shannon-Fisher feud in Evansville, Arkansas. Reed's brother Scott was killed by the Shannons for taking sides with the Fisher brothers along with his other former war associates, Frank James, Cole Younger and others. Reed revenged his brother's death by riding into Evansville one day in 1870 and killing two men who had supported the Shannons. This revenge required Reed to leave the territory. Sending his wife Belle and young daughter Pearl by stagecoach to California, Reed left on horseback. Meeting in California several weeks later, Jim and Belle Reed acquired a small farm where they hoped to spend the rest of their days as peaceful farmers. Their second child, Edwin, born in 1871, was named for Belle's brother Edwin Shirley who had been killed near Dallas at age sixteen.

After spending almost a year in relative peace in California, law authorities soon learned of Jim Reed's location and he had to leave hurriedly for Indian Territory. Belle returned to Texas by steamship with her two children.

In Dallas Belle renewed her horse fencing business. Being the known wife of a now highly wanted outlaw, Belle was constantly arrested on a variety of charges. Her father John Shirley was even arrested on one occasion and charged with harboring known outlaws. A citizens group was formed in Scyene who solicited help from Texas

Governor Coke to take action necessary to get such outlaw elements out of their city. Naturally Belle Reed, who considered herself to be very much a lady and honest business woman, became quite irate over such harassment of her family and threatened several members of the Scyene citizens committee. She warned them that if such harassment continued she would see to it that her outlaw friends burned them out.

Jim Reed was returning to Indian Territory after a secret meeting with Belle and his children on August 6, 1874. Who he felt was a trusted companion, John Morris, was riding with him. Morris suggested they stop by a rancher's home near Paris, Texas for a meal. He further explained that his rancher friend did not allow firearms being brought into his home, thus the two left their gun belts on their saddles. After a fine meal, Morris pretended to be helping the rancher by going to his well for a bucket of water. He returned to the house with his gun and killed Jim Reed in the rancher's home. Morris then took Reed's body to McKinney, Texas to claim the large reward posted for Reed. The sheriff there would not pay the reward until Reed's body could be positively identified. Belle Reed was notified. When Belle arrived she viewed the body and told the sheriff and Morris, "If you want to pay a reward for my husband Jim Reed, I suggest you kill Reed. This is not him." Naturally Morris did not get the reward. Reed's body was buried in an unmarked grave in McKinney. A few weeks later John Morris was shot and killed from ambush by an unknown party.

Tired of the continual harassment by her Scyene

and Dallas neighbors, Belle left Texas shortly after Jim Reed's death. Taking her children to live with their grandmother Reed in Rich Hill, Missouri, Belle began participating in major horse race events throughout Kansas, Missouri, and Arkansas border cities. Winning often with the fine string of horses she had accumulated in Texas, Belle's reputation continued to grow. Meeting Bruce Younger around the tracks, a close relationship developed as they traveled the racing circuit together. Records show that Belle and Bruce were married in Chetopa, Kansas on May 15, 1880. This marriage was a very brief one for it was only three weeks later that Belle returned to Jim Reed's old haunts in Indian Territory and married Sam Starr in a Cherokee ceremony. Thus Belle became Belle Starr.

Belle had apparently known the Starrs well from Jim Reed's past association with the Starr gang. Sam Starr had accompanied Reed on several trips to Dallas to bring Belle stolen horses to sell through her Dallas livery stable.

Shortly after Belle's marriage to Starr, Belle went to Missouri for her children and moved into the Starr cabin high on a ridge along the north banks of the south Canadian River in Indian Territory. Belle loved her new home and named it Youngers Bend in honor of Cole Younger who had been an old friend of the Shirley family and a person Belle highly admired for his service with Quantrill during the Civil War. The Starr cabin became a popular stopping place for outlaw bands as well as for deputy U. S. Marshalls riding through Indian Territory. Jesse and Frank James, the Youngers, the Daltons, and other outlaws and lawmen who

The Starr Cabin at Youngers Bend, Indian Territory.
Courtesy Oklahoma Historical Society.

Belle Reed, Younger, became Belle Starr

earned their place in western history were all known to take advantage of the hospitality Belle Starr provided at her Youngers Bend home.

Belle, being married to a Cherokee, strongly resented U. S. Marshalls riding out of Judge Isaac Parker's federal court in Fort Smith, continuing to interfere with Cherokee authorities in Indian Territory. Treaties the United States had made with the Cherokee Nation had given the Cherokees the right of authority over all crimes between Indians and between Indians and white adopted citizens within their nation. Belle, as well as Cherokee Nation leaders, therefore, felt such treaty rights were being violated when arrests were made by such Deputy Marshalls within the Cherokee Nation. Belle was found often in Fort Smith securing attorneys and arguing Cherokee treaty rights interpretation in Judge Parker's court for many of her Cherokee outlaw friends. During this period, Belle's unique appearance along Fort Smith streets with her pearl handled pistols over velvet dresses and the many news articles about her seeking help for Indian outlaws in Parker's jail earned her the designation of the Bandit Queen. Constantly seeking material for their publishers' deadlines, dime novel fiction writers found a new market by featuring Belle Starr as the leader of fictional outlaw gangs. Such early fiction writers therefore created the legend Belle Starr became and Belle, always having enjoyed showmanship and living in and around the outlaw circle, embellished such fictional stories about her.

Perhaps somewhat of a setup arranged by Judge Parker, about whom Belle was continually making

Belle Starr with Indian Outlaw friend Blue Duck

Federal Court Judge Isaac C. Parker

open comments around Fort Smith concerning his unfair treatment of Indian outlaws, stolen horses were found by marshalls at Youngers Bend. Sam and Belle were arrested on September 21, 1882 and sentenced to one year in prison at the Detroit House of Corrections on March 19, 1883. As a model prisoner, Belle became close friends with the warden's wife at the prison and was paroled after serving only nine months.

On Christmas eve in 1886, Sam and Belle Starr were returning to Youngers Bend from a Fort Smith shopping trip when they stopped by a Christmas party being held at a neighbor's farm. Sam joined a group of men who were sitting around an outdoor fire drinking homemade whiskey. Frank West was with the group. West, a member of the Cherokee Lighthorse Indian police agency, had been with a posse that fired at the Starr gang a few weeks before. Starr's favorite horse had been killed in the affair. Seeing West, Starr commented, "Why did you have to kill my horse?" West immediately pulled his gun and fired. Starr was mortally wounded, but also drew his weapon and killed West as he fell.

Belle took as her third husband a Cherokee some ten years younger than she named Jim July and remained at Youngers Bend. Since Belle Starr was by then somewhat of a legend as a result of the dime novels featuring her, Belle refused to take July's name. Rather, she forced July to change his name to Starr.

On Saturday morning, February 2, 1889, Belle left Youngers Bend with Jim July. July was riding to Fort Smith to answer a charge of horse theft in

Judge Parker's court. Spending the night at the home of Mrs. Nail near San Bois Creek, the next morning July rode on to Fort Smith alone. Belle had lunch and settled a bill at the King Creek store before returning to Youngers Bend on Sunday afternoon, February 3, 1889. She stopped by the home of Jackson Rowe, a neighbor, where several often gathered on Sunday afternoons. After visiting for awhile, she continued along the river road toward Youngers Bend. A short distance from the river crossing, Belle was shot in the back of the head from ambush. The assassin then ran to where she fell and shot her again in the chest and neck. The notorious Belle Starr was dead at age forty-one.

Belle was buried on the lawn in front of her home at her beloved Youngers Bend. A popular stone mason in the region designed the monument which featured a bell, horse, and star and created the most fitting epitaph for Belle's grave:

"Shed not for her
the bitter tear

Nor give the heart
to vain regret

Tis but the casket
that lies here

The gem that filled it
sparkles yet."

A major investigation was held to determine the identity of Belle's slayer. A neighbor, Edgar

Watson, was first accused. It was widely known that Belle and Watson did not like each other and that Belle had words with Watson only a few days before over Watson taking Belle's mail from the local post office at the Hoyt community. Watson had witnesses saying he was with them and, all other leads being circumstantial, Watson was acquitted and soon left Indian Territory for his native Florida.

Dr. Charles Mooney reported in his memoirs years later that Belle's son Eddie Reed told him he was going to kill his mother a few days before her murder. Belle had refused to let her son take her finest horse to a barn dance. Eddie took the horse anyway and, after staying gone a few days, returned home drunk. Belle went to the stable where she became irate after seeing the abuse Eddie had given her best racing mare. Returning to the cabin with a bull whip, Belle lashed her drunken son miserably. Crawling from the house, Eddie rode to Dr. Mooney for medical assistance and made the statement.

Jim Middleton, a noted Indian territory outlaw, was also suspected as Belle's possible assailant. Jim's brother, John "Rattlesnake" Middleton, had robbed Walt Grayson of several thousand dollars of Seminole Nation tribal funds. A short time later Middleton accompanied Belle and Jim July on a trip to Dardanelle, Arkansas. Middleton, fearing law authorities, left the Starrs at the Poteau River Crossing with plans to circle Fort Smith and meet them east of the city. Middleton never caught up with the Starrs and, a few months later, his remains washed out of the river bank. Jim Middleton openly accused the Starrs of killing his brother for the

Belle Starr's grave at Youngers Bend

Original monument featuring a bell, star, and horse that marked Belle Starr's grave

Seminole funds he was carrying and therefore was suspected as possibly being Belle's assassin.

Resulting from Belle always treating her husband Jim July as a child and frequently ordering him about, July was also a suspect in his wife's death. Since July was seen in Forth Smith, however, and time would not have permitted him to return to Youngers Bend in time, July was never officially charged. The identity of Belle Starr's assassin was never determined.

Belle's daughter Pearl Reed, with little formal education and with few jobs available for women, went to Fort Smith after her mother's death. There she became a lady of the evening. Soon her personality and popularity around the city enabled her to open her own bordello. Changing her name to Pearl Starr, taking advantage of her mother's popularity, Pearl became quite successful as a madam and acquired several pieces of real estate around this city. Although Pearl became quite popular around the city in business circles, pressures were brought to bear by the religious community to clean up the city. Forced to close her popular social club, Pearl left Fort Smith for Arizona where she remained until her death in 1925.

Pearl was survived by three daughters from several marriages whose descendents remain proud of their Belle Starr ancestry.

Belle's son Eddie Reed followed his outlaw father's profession for a short period. Judge Isaac Parker, perhaps attempting to help the boy, employed Eddie as a deputy U. S. Marshall after Eddie served only a few months in prison for a horse theft charge. Eddie married a school teacher. A short time afterward, while attempting to close down a Claremore saloon for poisoning his father-in-law, Eddie was killed on December 14, 1896.

Pearl Starr, Belle Starr's only daughter, with two of her daughters - Ruth Kaigler (standing) and Jeannette Steele Andrews

Chapter 6

Billy The Kid

Henry McCarty, Henry Antrim, Billy Bonney, Billy the Kid

Perhaps second only to Jesse James in the numbers of articles, books, and films about them, Billy the Kid remains at the top of the list of unearned significance in Old West history and folklore. Little is known of his early life other than the fact he was born as Henry McCarty to Catherine McCarty in New York City on November 23, 1859. He had an older brother named Joseph, whom the family called Josie. Nothing is known of their natural father. It is assumed that Catherine McCarty left New York with her two sons in 1866 in search of a better climate since she suffered from tuberculosis. Settling in Marion County, Indiana Catherine soon met William H. Antrim from Huntsville, Indiana whom she was to eventually marry. In 1869 Catherine took her two boys along with Mr. Antrim to Kansas. They settled near Coffeyville for a short time before moving on to Wichita. There Antrim took employment as a farm laborer, as a carpenter, and as a part time bartender.

Records further indicate that Antrim joined thousands of others who rushed to Colorado to prospect for gold in 1871. By 1873 the couple had left Colorado to prospect for silver in New Mexico. Catherine and William Antrim were finally married in Sante Fe, New Mexico on March 1, 1873. Records indicate that Henry and Josie McCarty were witnesses to the wedding. Catherine's tuberculosis, or Antrim's obsession for finding wealth, shows they moved soon after to Silver City, New Mexico. Catherine's illness continued to get worse and she died of what was then called "galloping consumption" on September 16, 1874. Her son Henry was age fourteen at the time of his mother's death.

After his mother's death, for some reason, Henry left his father and brother Josie to live with Mr. and Mrs. Del Truesdale, parents of his schoolmate friend, Chauncey Truesdale. The Truesdales operated the Star Hotel and boarding house. There Henry earned his room and board by waiting on tables, washing dishes, and doing other chores around the hotel. Later, after William Antrim secured employment in a Silver City butcher shop, he boarded with Richard Knight, the shop's owner, and Henry joined his brother and stepfather there. Antrim then took employment at a mill in Georgetown, New Mexico. Henry couldn't leave due to school so he boarded with a Mrs. Brown.

Until this time, Henry McCarty had been a likable, honest boy around Silver City. His first trouble seems to have been in 1875 when the youth was arrested for stealing clothes from a Chinese laundry owned by Charley and Sam Chung. Although the episode was more of a prank than a crime, Sheriff Harvey Whitehall, no doubt hoping to teach Henry a lesson, jailed him.

If one were to single out any one attribute of Henry McCarty (Billy the Kid) or reason he obtained so much notoriety, it might be for his uncanny ability to escape from almost any jail. Henry, though surely realizing the trouble over the laundry theft was a minor charge, simply had a phobia for being incarcerated. Rather than sit behind bars to await action being taken, Henry somehow managed to squeeze his way up the jail's chimney and strike out for Arizona.

No doubt because of his youthful appearance,

and fear that he might be still wanted for the laundry theft incident, he chose to use the name Antrim in Arizona. There the ranch hands on the W. J. Smith ranch began calling him Kid Antrim when he first took employment there.

The first man killed by the Kid, of the some twenty-one legend says he killed before his twenty-first birthday, was a blacksmith named Cahill. Billy the Kid, though certainly not handsome, apparently had an engaging personality that appealed to young women of the region. It also has been said that he was a good dancer and often frequented dance halls. On August 17, 1877 he went to such a dance hall in the Bonito community with some of his ranchhand friends. Somehow a quarrel erupted between the Kid and Cahill. Cahill called the boy a "pimp" which resulted in a brawl. The large and strong blacksmith had no problem overpowering the youth. During the struggle, the Kid grabbed one of Cahill's guns and shot him through the stomach as they were struggling. A Justice of the Peace decided the shooting was criminal and not justifiable and that Henry Antrim, alias the Kid, was guilty. Arrested while eating breakfast in a hotel the next morning, the Kid was taken peaceably to the post guardhouse at nearby Camp Grant and jailed. Somehow, while a social function was in progress at the camp, young Antrim managed to once again escape.

Grabbing a fast horse, the Kid rode to the Knight Ranch some forty miles south of Silver City. There he had many friends and could have remained but chose two weeks later to leave for Mesilla, New Mexico. Henry was now calling himself Billy Antrim.

In Mesilla, Billy joined up with a youth his age,

Tom O'Keefe. Riding through the Organ Mountains, O'Keefe stole Antrim's bedroll and horse while Antrim was climbing down in a canyon to get water for his canteen. Left alone with no horse, Antrim walked through the mountains to the ranch of Heiskell and Ma'am Jones who lived there with ten children. Antrim had not eaten for several days and the Joneses took him in. There, Henry McCarty, Billy Antrim, first introduced himself to the Joneses as being Billy Bonney. Just from where Billy chose to use the Bonney name is not known. No family relationship to such a name has ever been determined and it therefore is assumed it was simply a sudden choice to use in concealing his true identity. After recuperating several days, he borrowed a horse from the hospitable Jones family and rode to Lincoln County, New Mexico. His first stop after leaving the Joneses was at John Chisum's South Spring River Ranch where he was made welcome. He was not hired, but stayed several weeks. He became friends there with several cowhands, several of whom were known rustlers, one of whom was Dick Brewer. Brewer was hired by a rancher named Tunstill to be his ranch foreman while Tunstill looked after his general store and bank enterprises in Lincoln, New Mexico. In January of 1878 Tunstill hired the Kid to work for him on his Rio Feliz Ranch.

On February 18, 1878 John Tunstill, the twenty-five year old son of the London merchant who had come west to seek his fortune, was driving a small herd of horses near the Ruidoso River. As the riders rode through the scrub brush, several wild turkeys fluttered away. Tunstill sent two of his men after the turkeys. Suddenly the remaining four men were surrounded and split into two groups by a group of riders firing their weapons and riding hard. Jesse Evans, Billy Morton, and Tom Hill confronted Tunstill in a patch of scrub oak and sent a slug into Tunstill's chest. Another shot to the back of his head knocked Tunstill to the ground. The men then dismounted and bashed Tunstill's skull with a rifle butt and then shot Tunstill's horse. The men then took Tunstill's gun and fired two rounds which would prove Tunstill had resisted.

The southwest quadrant of the New Mexico quadrant bordering Texas had been controlled for years by cattleman Major Lawrence Murphy. Murphy, with Sheriff William Brady in his pocket, had controlled government contracts for goods at Fort Stanton and the Indian reservation for years. Through his store in Lincoln, Murphy managed to prevent competition by controlling prices for supplies. Murphy turned control of his empire over to James Dolan and John Riley who were to continue to dominate the New Mexico territory cattle industry.

John Chism, Tunstill, and Alexander McSween, a Lincoln attorney, joined forces to put a stop to the devious attempts the Murphy empire was using to squeeze other ranchers out of the territory. Tunstill built a store and opened a bank in Lincoln which treated the small ranchers more fairly. McSween directed his legal harassment toward the Murphy-Dolan faction for their continual rustling and other attempts to destroy competing small ranchers in the territory. Dolan reacted to the Chism, Tunstill, McSween alliance by hiring a gang of outlaws to prey on the Chism and Tunstill interests. Dolan trumped up a dubious embezzlement charge against

McSween and encouraged their controlled Sheriff Brady to form a posse to arrest Tunstill. The posse, being made up of outlaws Dolan had hired, then ran down Tunstill and killed him.

Billy the Kid liked Tunstill better than any other man in his life. Tunstill had given the youth a new horse and saddle when the Kid first went to work for him and in spite of his youth always treated the Kid as a man. The Kid was therefore very upset over the death of his boss and swore to run down and kill all of Tunstill's killers. The next day the Lincoln Justice of the Peace, Billy the Kid, and another ranch hand went to the Dolan-Murphy store with warrants for Tunstill's killers. Sheriff Brady was there and arrested the trio. Taking the Kid's rifle, Brady jailed him for a short period. When released, the trio went to Tunstill's foreman, Dick Brewer, and they formed a group of a dozen men which they called "the Regulators". Dedicated to running down all of those with the party that had killed Tunstill, the group eventually grew to sixty men. All of the small ranchers of the territory supported the Regulators' efforts against the power of the Dolan-Murphy empire.

On March 9, 1878, Billy the Kid and other Regulators tracked down Billy Morton. Disregarding Dick Brewer's orders to take him alive, the Kid and others gunned down Morton and a companion who had also been with the party that killed Tunstill.

The Dolan-Murphy faction soon used their power with the territorial governor in Sante Fe to declare the Regulators to be outlaws. Warrants for their arrest and a $200 reward for the capture of any Regulator was then issued.

Billy the Kid and three other Regulators silently rode into Lincoln on March 31. Hiding in an adobe corral, they waited until they saw Sheriff Brady and three other Dolan men walking down the street. Brady was carrying the rifle he had previously taken from the Kid. Billy the Kid opened fire on the party, killing Brady. George Hindman was also killed. The Kid and one of his companions were slightly wounded but managed to get out of town before other Dolan men could come after them.

Three days later the Regulators tracked down Andrew "Buckshot" Roberts, another of the party who had killed Tunstill. In the ensuing gun fight, Roberts was mortally wounded but Dick Brewer, the leader of the Regulators was killed by a bullet in the head from Roberts' gun. Brewer was age twenty-five at his death and was buried alongside his enemy Roberts on a hill overlooking their Mescalero reservation battleground.

Frank McNab, who had been looking after Chism's herd while Brewer was riding with the Regulators, took Brewer's place as leader of the Regulators upon Brewer's death. Shortly afterward a Dolan posse bushwhacked McNab and then decided to move against the Regulators' headquarters at McSween's Lincoln home. The Lincoln County War came to an end in July of 1878. McSween, learning of Dolan's plans, gathered some 50 to 60 Regulators around his Lincoln home. Dispersing themselves along the town's main street, inside the McSween home and Tunstill store, they waited for the Dolan party.

Dolan's party of some forty men arrived in Lincoln on the afternoon of July 15. Gun fire was exchanged back and forth between the factions throughout the day with the only casualties being a horse and a mule.

The next day the U.S. Army stepped in. Although legally the Army was barred from using troops as a posse in civil disturbances, Lt. Colonel Nathan Dudley felt morally justified in trying to bring peace to the region.

The army was however fired upon repeatedly by both sides causing numerous casualties. McSween received a fatal hit. Two other Regulators also joined McSween in death as the firing continued throughout the day on July 16. Billy the Kid had been instrumental in the slaying of two Dolan men. Nothing was settled between the parties in those two days of warfare. The battle was, however, the dissolution of the Regulators as an organized band.

Billy the Kid, following some kind of confrontation with John Chism, then took some of his die-hard Regulator companions to rustle some of Chism's cattle. The Kid and his closest companions, Charlie Bowdre and Tom O'Folliard, attempted to get a gubernatorial pardon from New Mexico territorial governor Lew Wallace in Santa Fe, but it was not to be.

The group then had few places to turn other than rustling for survival as they were wanted men for their Regulator activities.

Chism and Dolan somehow peaceably settled their differences and together they were instrumental in getting 30 year old Pat Garrett elected Sheriff of Lincoln County on a law and order platform. Upon his election, Garrett, who had known

Billy Bonney and his associates, set out immediately to bring in this remaining outlaw faction of the Regulators. On December 13 Governor Wallace announced a $500 reward for Bonney, alias "The Kid."

On the bitterly cold morning of December 19, Garrett's posse ambushed the Kid and five of his followers near Fort Sumner. Tom O'Folliard was mortally wounded. The others escaped. Garrett's party followed them some twenty-five miles eastward to an old shepherd's stone hut at Stinking Springs.

Two days before Christmas, Charlie Bowdre emerged from the hut at early dawn. A volley of rifle bullets from Garrett's posse knocked him back through the doorway. Hopelessly surrounded and hungry, Billy Bonney and his gang surrendered later that day. Garrett chained the party into the back of an army wagon and returned them to Lincoln. The Kid was convicted of murdering Sheriff Brady and sentenced to hang. Irregardless of his guilt, Billy Bonney was the only member of the Regulators or participant in the Lincoln County War to be convicted of any crime.

Bonney was placed on the second floor of the county courthouse which had formerly been Dolan's old store. Jim Bell and Bob Olinger were placed to guard Bonney. On April 28, while Olinger was escorting other prisoners across the street for supper at the Worley Hotel, Bonney asked the remaining guard if he could use the outhouse behind the courthouse. Somehow when returning from the outhouse, Bonney had slipped out of his handcuffs. Reaching the courthouse, Bonney surprised Jim Bell by grabbing a shotgun and killing him. Running upstairs, Bonney then grabbed Olinger's shotgun and positioned himself at the northeast window. Hearing the shot, Olinger ran back toward the courthouse. Bonney yelled at Olinger to look up just as he fired both barrels, taking the life of Olinger. Grabbing a mining pick, he quickly severed his leg irons and grabbed a horse on the street. Riding up to Olinger's body, the Kid dropped Olinger's rifle alongside the body and rode out of town.

This daring escape, two weeks before he was to be hanged for a crime many citizens felt he should not have been singly charged with, made national newspaper headlines throughout the nation and the legend of this daring New Mexico youth began.

Garrett hurriedly organized a posse to track down this little buck-toothed youth who had greatly damaged his pride. He tracked the Kid's movements over a period of three month's. Finally, on the night of July 14, 1881, Garrett found Billy on the Maxwell ranch. As Garrett explained in his memoirs, he entered a darkened bedroom of the Maxwell ranch house that opened on the front of the house and sat on the bed while his possemen waited outside. Billy, hearing noises as he moved down the porch yelled out, "Who is it?" in Spanish. Billy was carrying a knife and a pistol when he backed into the darkened room. Garrett explained that the Kid turned toward him just as Garrett fired two shots at the Kid's shadowy figure. "I had no alternative but to kill him, or suffer death at his hands," Garrett later replied. Henry McCarty, Billy Antrim, Billy the Kid, was killed instantly.

Due to the circumstances of the Kid's death,

Pat Garrett (left) with friends James Brent and John Poe, 1884

many citizens ridiculed Garrett and insinuated that Garrett didn't have the nerve to face the Kid. A coroner's jury, however, acquitted Garrett's act as being justifiable homicide.

Billy the Kid was buried first at the Maxwell ranch. Later, to avoid the thousands of curious souvenir hunters, the Kid's body was moved to a common grave near Fort Sumner where it was placed with the bodies of his two former friends, Tom O'Folliard and Charlie Bowdre. The word "Pals" was later etched into the monument marking their graves.

Pat Garrett's life was greatly effected over the controversial manner in which he killed Billy the Kid. Garrett was killed by an angry tenant working his land on February 29, 1908.

Caught up in a set of circumstances in a relatively lawless land in which cattle barons formed their own laws, Billy the Kid no doubt felt justified in his support of the Regulators against those who had killed his friend Tunstill. As the tide of history turned to the government supporting the Dolan faction during the Lincoln County War, and warrants were issued for those who served with the Regulators, Billy the Kid had no place to turn. Had Billy the Kid first stopped at the Dolan-Murphy empire for employment when he ran from Silver City to escape his laundry theft prank charge, it is doubtful there would have ever been a Billy the Kid. Arguments among historians of the Old West as to whether the Kid was a ruthless killer or simply an innocent youth caught up with a group of cowhands seeking revenge for their boss's death will no doubt always continue. Such were the circumstances of the period, his youth, uncanny ability to escape confinement, and newspaper headlines that led many a dime novel fiction writer to create the legend of Billy the Kid.

John D. LeVan, left, composed and performs the original songs on the album that accompanies Outlaws and Gunfighters. Author, Phillip W. Steele, right.